YOUR
PRIME
MINISTER
IS DEAD

YOUR PRIME MINISTER IS DEAD

ANUJ DHAR

Vitasta

Published by
Renu Kaul Verma
Vitasta Publishing Pvt Ltd
4348/4C, Ansari Road, Daryaganj
New Delhi - 110 002
info@vitastapublishing.com

ISBN 978-93-86473-35-6

First Edition 2019
14th Reprint 2025
MRP ₹450

Editor Veena Batra
Cover and layout by Somesh Kumar Mishra
Printed by Vikas Computer and Printers

Contents

Prologue

When a devastating earthquake shook Tashkent in April 1966, leaving scores dead and more than 300 thousand out of 1.5 million residents homeless, some God-fearing survivors felt it was a divine retribution for what had happened to the Indian prime minister earlier that year. A few months afterwards, a tearful Lalita Shastri visited the quaint villa where her husband had been lodged. A lady caretaker guided her to the room where he had breathed his last. The Uzbeki woman's eyebrows wrinkled. 'No telephone,' she sombrely whispered—underlining that the Indian PM was virtually cut off from the world when his last moments came.

The suspicions that some people in Tashkent spoke about in hushed tones were the talk of the town in India in those days. That there was something more to Lal Bahadur Shastri's death than what had been given out officially. Today, the tragedy in Tashkent ranks as one of India's two most enduring political controversies, the other being the disappearance of Netaji Subhas Chandra Bose. So overwhelming is the spectre of Shastri's death on our collective psyche that every time his name is taken, the discussion invariably leads to what really happened in January 1966. Shastri's great life needs no elaboration. His simplicity, honesty and integrity are forever etched on our minds, but gnawing at our conscious still is the nagging question why there never was an inquiry into the only instance in our history where our head of government had died in a foreign land?

It's not that the matter was not flagged before the nation. Moments after Shastriji's obituary was read out in Parliament, Atal Bihari Vajpayee asked: 'What really happened in Tashkent?' He wondered if Shastri's death could have been avoided. Why couldn't he summon his doctor from his bed when he felt uncomfortable? Why wasn't there provision for administering oxygen in his room? If there was a proper arrangement, his life perhaps could have been saved in those crucial 5-6 minutes.

But then, who would have wanted Shastri dead? What could have been the motive for even contemplating such a horrendous crime against India? In the words of his childhood friend TN Singh, Shastri was *ajatshatru*—'hardly any enemy could be born to that man'. A Central

Intelligence Agency assessment of 1965 agreed: 'He has made very few enemies in a 40-year career in politics'.

There was no inquiry because the official stand was always firm that Shastriji had died due to a heart attack. There was absolutely nothing to suspect foul play. Some people alleged that there was something, but nothing would convince those in power to take a relook at the official position. The demands that were raised off and on died out and the issue went into cold storage. It was intermittently revived along with the Subhas Bose controversy. As it happened, both matters became intertwined. As the followers of Bose succeeded in compelling the Government to conduct a judicial probe into the matter in 1970, Shastri's followers (including those who were agitating over the Bose issue as well) made their best ever pitch. All went in vain. For all practical purposes, the case ceased to be a major issue from that year.

So why are we interested in it in 2018? What purpose would this slim volume serve so many years after the tragedy occurred? My basic purpose is to try and get a proper closure that was denied in those days. There are so many people who still want to have it, especially the members of Shastriji's family for whom it's a tragedy they are still grappling with. His two surviving sons' eyes turn misty still when they are asked to think back to that horrifying night when the phone rang and they were told that Shastri was seriously ill. For the next 30 minutes or so, led by a devout Lalita Shastri, they prostrated in prayer before the deities, but…

For years I ignored the suggestions that after having written books about the Subhas Chandra Bose death controversy, I should attempt one on the Shastri matter. There were two reasons I did not go with these suggestions. First, unlike the Bose matter, the Shastri death issue did not have much by way of official records. My own RTI applications (first ever filed by anyone concerning the Shastri death issue) fetched me information sufficient only to inspire news stories and articles. While they are discussed in the same breath, both Netaji and Shastriji cases are dissimilar in one respect: The opponents of the official theory claimed that Netaji was alive after his reported death, whereas Shastriji's life did end in Tashkent. So there was much more to explore in the former case than the latter. In the Shastri matter, it was all about making sure that his end was natural. To create a concise, cogent narrative around it in the absence of sufficient reference material was an uphill task.

The second reason I did not want to do this book was because I was wary of getting typecast as someone who writes about the deaths of national icons, even though my motive is to seek a resolution of such cases. So, even though I wrote some of the most well-read articles on the

Shastri case, I had no inclination to attempt a book on the matter until this year.

It was during a lunch with filmmaker Vivek Agnihotri a few months back at a Delhi hotel that the idea of writing this book first crossed my mind. It is the making of Agnihotri's upcoming film *The Tashkent Files*—for which I have provided research inputs— which fired my imagination. I overcame my inhibitions because of an overpowering urge to do more, charged up by the prospect of this movie creating an atmosphere conducive for the final settlement of this issue of national importance.

ONE

Death strikes silently

IF THERE IS anything such as an angel of death, he was quietly lurking somewhere in a corner in Tashkent even as everything seemed to move around Lal Bahadur Shastri. He and his Pakistani counterpart, General Ayub Khan, were lodged in two different villas, or dachas as they are called in that part of the world. Running back and forth between them like an errand boy was Soviet premier Alexei Kosygin, more suave of the two leaders[1] in charge of the second most powerful nation in the world at that time.

The chilly morning of 10 January 1966 heralded a warm conclusion to the never ending parleys between Indian and Pakistani delegates for seven consecutive days.

1 The other being Leonid Brezhnev, General Secretary of the Central Committee of the Communist Party of the Soviet Union (CPSU). Kosygin was Chairman of the USSR Council of Ministers.

If you could somehow be transported there back in time, you would see Shastri with no sign of any strain on his smiling face. To the eyes of CP Srivastava, member of the Indian delegation, Shastri appeared 'beaming'. So full of life he was that one could have not believed that he had by this time suffered two minor heart attacks, the last one occurring in 1964. But then, as an assessment made by the Central Intelligence Agency (CIA) that very year reveals, he was 'a fully recovered cardiac patient'. As late as 31 December 1965, Shastri was thoroughly examined by doctors in Delhi and declared fit.

The Tashkent agreement between India and Pakistan was signed around 4 pm in full glare of officials and media. All eyes followed the Indian and Pakistani heads of government. Shastri, of light frame and under five feet tall, amusingly looked up at an imposing Ayub Khan sporting a petit handlebar moustache in contrast to his unassuming persona. As they began to shake hands vigorously, everyone clapped. History was made. At around 8 pm both had joined a reception hosted in their honour by Kosygin. The evening was very lively; there was music, dance and good food. Shastri continued to look quite well. He carried himself with his usual ease throughout. Foreign Secretary, CS Jha, saw him chatting with Ayub Khan in an atmosphere that was 'though not overly convivial [but] was good'. After 9 pm, Shastri, Foreign Minister Swaran Singh and Defence Minister YB Chavan left the reception.

Around 10 pm, Shastri reached the dacha where he had been lodged by his Soviet hosts. It was located at some distance from the Intourist Hotel where other members of the Indian Delegation and journalists were lodged. The PM was obviously not alone in the dacha. Accompanying him were his personal physician Dr RN Chugh, security officer R Kapur, private secretary JN Sahai, personal assistant MMN Sharma and Ram Nath, personal attendant. Chugh had been attached to Shastri since 1955, and Ram Nath was working with Shastri's family for more than twenty years. He was in charge of all of Shastri's personal belongings. He also used to work in the kitchen to help in the preparation of Shastri's food. Shastri went to his suite on the ground floor. It comprised a bedroom, a bathroom and a study. Adjoining the study was a reception room for the visitors. Next to the reception room on the opposite side was a bedroom allotted to Dr Chugh and R Kapur. The first floor had two rooms where Sharma and Ram Nath were lodged along with Mohammed Jan, the cook for the Indian Ambassador in Moscow.

After Shastri had changed, Ram Nath enquired about

his dinner. At first Shastri did not want anything as he had eaten something at the reception, but then he asked for something light. Ram Nath went to kitchen on the ground floor and brought a dish of spinach and potatoes and a curry prepared by Mohammed Jan, helped by Russian cooks. Having had it, Shastri went to his study, where Sahai came to see him to discuss the schedule for the next day. At this time, (10.20 pm, corresponding to 9.50 pm IST), there was a telephone call from the Prime Minister's residence in New Delhi. Jawaharlal Nehru as India's first prime minister had taken up residence at the palatial Teen Murti House, built as the home of the second most powerful man in the British Raj era—the Commander-in-Chief of the British Indian Army. Shastri's office was located at 10 Janpath. But he and his family stayed in the adjoining 1, Motilal Nehru Marg bungalow, which was connected to 10 Janpath through a corridor.

Sahai received the call from VS Venkataraman, the Prime Minister's Private Secretary, who enquired whether Shastri had any particular wishes regarding the arrangements to be made for his reception at New Delhi airport on his return. Sahai conveyed this to Shastri. Never a fussy boss, Shastri said they should do whatever they considered appropriate.

While Sahai and Venkataraman were still on the

telephone, Shastri asked about the reaction to the Tashkent accord back home. Sahai put this question to Venkataraman, who replied that the declaration had been generally well received, except that Atal Bihari Vajpayee and SN Dwivedy were somewhat critical. Shastri's reaction to this, as per Sahai's account to CP Srivastava, was: 'They are in the Opposition and it is their right to be critical.'[2]

There was a second call from Delhi during which Shastri spoke with his family members. He wanted to have a word with his wife but since the sound quality was poor, he conversed with VN Singh, his younger son-in-law. Lal Bahadur and Lalita had six children. Kusum and Suman were elder to brothers Hari Krishna, Anil, Sunil and Ashoke. Apart from Anil and Sunil, all others are deceased. During the course of his talk with his son-in law, his last interaction with his family, Shastri tried to gauge the public mood over the Tashkent accord.

It was nearing midnight. Prem Vaidya of the Films Division (now reckoned as a legend in the field of documentary film making), was wanting to take shots of the PM. After obtaining permission a little earlier, he and two more journalists were observing Shastri from

---

2 CP Srivastava, **Lal Bahadur Shastri: A Life of Truth in Politics**, Oxford University Press.

outside the dacha. 'The view from the dark outside into the lighted room through a French window and a lone figure moving around in silhouette', Vaidya would write in his memoirs published in 2009 by the National Film Archive of India. For posterity, he captured haunting last visuals of Shastri pacing in the dacha.

When Shastri retired to his bedroom, Ram Nath, following the daily routine, gave him some milk with Isabgol. The milk had been boiled in the kitchen by Ram Nath himself. The Prime Minister paced up and down for a while, brooding about something. After a while, he asked for water. Ram Nath gave some from the flask kept in his bedroom. He stayed with the PM till half past midnight, when Shastri asked him to leave. He put out the lights and left the suite.

Sahai had in the meanwhile returned to the staff bedroom. Together with MMN Sharma, Dr Chugh and Security Officer Kapur, he had completed the packing of the luggage. Dr Chugh had gone to sleep. This was 1.20 am on 11 January and Sahai, Sharma and Kapur had no clue about the nightmare that was already unfolding in the Prime Minister's bedroom. Just as they were about to put off the lights, they heard something moving. Then all of a sudden the Prime Minister most unexpectedly appeared at their door. He was in his nightwear, and he looked greatly distressed. 'Doctor,' he murmured in a feeble voice and turned his back on them. It took the staff a fraction of second to sense that something was terribly wrong. They sprang towards Shastri and held him. Sahai ran out to wake up Dr Chugh.

Hardly had Shastri walked the few steps back to his room helped by Sharma and Kapur when he started coughing. With difficulty he reached his bed and was made to lie down. The coughing became so intense that he started gasping for breath. He sat up and held his chest with his hands. His face turned pallid. '*Oh mere Ram*' was all he said repeatedly. He pointed to the flask of water kept next to his bed.

Dr Chugh rushed in at this juncture. He found Shastri's pulse to be very fast but feeble. Blood pressure could not be registered. The heartbeats were hardly audible. The PM was having a massive heart attack. Chugh panicked. Quickly, he put Shastri in a reclining position and administered an intra-muscular injection of Mepthentin Sulphate one ml (15 mgm) and one ml of Micorena. There was no effect. Within the next three minutes Shastri lost consciousness, his pulse disappeared, breathing stopped and the heartbeats could not be heard. Dr Chugh immediately began the revival treatment by indirect massage of the heart and artificial respiration through the mouth by means of an air-tube. But he was distraught by now. '*Babuji, aap ne mujhe mouka nahin diya*,' he wailed. (Babuji, you did not give me a chance).

This was 1.32 am in Tashkent. In India, it was a little past 1 am and the nation slept unaware of the tragedy that had just struck.

The Soviet doctor on duty entered the room. Prof Evgenia Yeremenko too found that Shastri had no pulse. His heart was silent and there was no breath and no corneal reflexes. In the next few minutes, a team of senior doctors led by Dr Uktam Aripovich Aripov, Deputy Minister of Health of Uzbekistan, took charge of the situation. They started revival treatment. Indirect massage of the heart was done; in the left cavity under the heart a mixture of calcium chloride with adrenalin and glucose was introduced twice at an interval of fifteen minutes. Artificial respiration by means of the machine with the help of 'Intubation tube' was also attempted. But more than an hour-long effort to revive Shastri went in vain.

By this time, the word had gone around in Intourist Hotel. Fatigued, CS Jha was half asleep when he was woken by agitated, loud voices of Swaran Singh and Ambassador TN Kaul coming from the corridor. Kuldip Nayar, Shastri's media advisor was in for a shock he would never fully recover from. He was rudely awoken by frantic loud thumps. He opened the door to find a Russian lady telling him, 'Your Prime Minister is dying.' Fellow journalist Prem Prakash (now chairman of news agency ANI) had it even worse. The telephone rang in the middle of the night. The caller at the other end dropped the bombshell. 'Your Prime Minister is dead. Please come down as soon as you can.'[3] When Kuldip Nayar reached the dacha, he saw Kosygin standing in the verandah with a look on his face that portended a disaster. He walked past him and saw Russian doctors in confabulation with Dr RN Chugh in the dining room. His heart in his mouth, Nayar went inside and saw Shastri crumpled on the huge bed. His face had shrivelled but was serene as in life. His slippers were in place on the carpeted floor. But the dressing table was overturned and it appeared to Nayar as if Shastri had struggled with the thermos.

Nayar asked Dr Chugh what had happened and he just said, 'Shastriji did not give me time.' Sahai told him that Shastri had come to their door past midnight. 'It was a heart attack and this walk was fatal,' Dr Chugh said.

3 **"Come down your Prime Minister is dead"—A first hand account of the night PM Shastri Died.** Accessed from https://www.aninews.in/news/national/general-news/come-down-your-prime-minister-is-dead-a-first-hand-account-of-the-night-pm-shastri-died201801111841140001/.

Foreign Secretary Jha had arrived when the Soviet doctors were still making futile attempts to revive Shastri. He saw Swaran Singh and Chavan standing transfixed in shock. According to Jha, once the doctors gave up, a telegram was sent by Swaran Singh and Chavan to President Radhakrishnan in Delhi. However, then Home Secretary LP Singh would write that the onerous task fell on his shoulders as protocol required: "Home Secretary to inform various authorities about the death of the holder of any high office of state". After failing to get anyone on phone at the Rashtrapti Bhawan, he called the Home Minister's residence and got though to Gulzarilal Nanda quickly. Genial-looking Nanda was shell-shocked.

The words Kosygin uttered after Shastri was gone were: 'The world has lost one of its greatest leaders.' By 3.30 am, General Ayub walked in. To both Jha and Nayar, he appeared genuinely grieved. 'Here is a man of peace who gave his life for amity between India and Pakistan,' he said. In time, more tributes poured in. US President Lyndon Johnson said Shastri's death was a 'grievous blow to the hopes of mankind for peace and progress.' Pope John Paul said he was 'profoundly saddened' by Shastri's demise 'during his mission of pacification.' Queen Elizabeth spoke of a 'sense of loss which will be felt throughout the world.'

With the breaking of dawn preparations were underway to send Shastri's body to India. At 9.30 am Tashkent time, the body, draped in the Tricolour, was put in a wooden coffin and placed on a gun carriage. Followed by cars carrying Kosygin, Uzbek premier Kushanov, Foreign Minister Swaran Singh and Defence Minister Chavan, the procession left for the airport. The entire route of 17 kilometers was lined with countless shocked locals, who had braved freezing temperatures to bid goodbye to their guest.

At the airport, thousands watched as the coffin was carried into the aircraft with Swaran Singh, Chavan, Ayub Khan and Kosygin turning pall bearers. As CS Jha bid Ayub goodbye, he said, '*Jha Saheb, yeh kya ho gaya? Khuda na karen iska nateeja hamare mulkon per bura ho.*' (Mr Jha, what a terrible thing to happen? God forbid that the consequences of this tragedy are harmful for our countries).[4] Jha was moved.

The Soviet Aeroflot Illushin-18 plane carrying Shastri's body landed at Palam airport at 2.31 pm IST. Swaran Singh and Chavan emerged from it first and then conducted PM's weeping eldest son, Hari Kishan

4 CS Jha, **From Bandung to Tashkent: Glimpses of India's Foreign Policy**, Sangam Books, 1983.

Shastri, into the plane. After half an hour, Shastri's body was moved out of the airport in a gun carriage used for the funeral of Pandit Nehru. By the time it reached 10 Janpath at 4.10 pm, the procession was nearly a mile long. As in Tashkent, but in far bigger numbers, countless people had stood in silence on both sides of the roads from the airport to Lutyens' Delhi. It was an unimaginable nightmare. Less than two years after Jawaharlal Nehru departed, his successor too was gone, barely hours after hogging international limelight.

TWO

Controversy erupts

ALL INSTANCES OF unexpected deaths are received with a sense of disbelief. In the case of Lal Bahadur Shastri, it was all the more because he had died far away from home. Disbelief soon turned into suspicions. These began to be spoken about in hushed tones by the dead Prime Minister's near and dear ones. From them, the word went around the country like wildfire. The first sign that a controversy was building up came just after Shastri's obituary was read out in Parliament. In Rajya Sabha on 14 February, Atal Bihari Vajpayee was the first to lament (probably because the kind-hearted Jan Sangh leader was carrying a burden on his conscience that his harsh criticism of the Tashkent pact might have hurt Shastri on the last day of his life), 'Why couldn't Shastri summon his personal staff from his bed?'

On 16th, Swaran Singh made the first statement about the PM's death. He admitted that in Tashkent all looked well till the last moment. 'My colleague, the Defence Minister, and I, as well as other members of the delegation were constantly with him for long periods every day,' he said. 'He was cheerful and relaxed. His daily schedule of work was less strenuous than it was in Delhi, and at no time did he complain of being unwell, or in fact, show any signs of fatigue or strain.' The minister added that all the arrangements for Shastri's stay in Tashkent were made 'in consultation with and under the supervision of our Ambassador in Moscow.' The minister placed on record 'our thanks and appreciation to the Government of the USSR' for all that they did 'for the comfort and convenience of the late Prime Minister' before the tragedy struck.

Then, in response to a pointed query why there was no telephone in Shastri's room, Singh clarified that there actually were 'two telephones for internal and international calls fitted in the Prime Minister's suite.' There was also a third telephone, he added, with a buzzer which could be activated by simply lifting the receiver. 'This instrument was available for the Prime Minister's use to call any member of his personal staff or the doctor in case of need.'

The minister went on to place on record a medical report signed by Dr Chugh and six other Soviet doctors. The report too stated that during all the days of his stay in Tashkent, as well as on the evening of 10th January, Shastri "felt well" and "never complained about his health". But, as it happened, he suddenly passed away on early 11th morning. The report concluded:

> Taking into account the fact that Prime Minister LB Shastri had suffered even in the past from infarkt miokarda [myocardial infarction] and the fact that during the night from 10th to 11th of January, 1966, there was an acute attack of the same disease, it can be considered that death occurred because of an acute attack of infarkt miokarda.

Any thoughts that this would stem the doubts were short-lived. Joining the issue with the foreign minister, Atal Bihari Vajpayee pointedly asked who gave Shastri the glass of milk. By this time, Mohammed Jan was being treated as a suspect by Shastri's family and friends. 'It was reported from Tashkent by Indian correspondents that the last thing that Shastriji took was a glass of milk. I should like to know who was the person who offered that glass of milk?'

'I cannot say that because the service was always done by Shri Ram Nath, the attendant. I do not know whether he took milk as the last thing and I do not know who administered it,' responded Swaran Singh, who had no clear answer. Vajpayee pressed: 'Let the Minister find out whether a glass of milk was offered to Shastriji before he went to sleep. I want that information; I do not want any deduction from that information but the honourble Minister must be in a position to deny or confirm it.' Swaran Singh duly responded: 'I cannot deny or confirm it because I do not have any information as to what was the last thing that he took and who gave it to him. If the honourble Member is interested, I will try to find out. In a matter like this, I would submit that we are dealing with the wishes of the Prime Minister of the country, and what arrangement could I or anyone else make? He is the best judge. The doctor is there in the same building. His attendant is there. There is a buzzer in the room; as soon as he lifts it, there is a buzzing sound in the room of his attendant, in the room of the doctor and in the room of his assistants. All of them will come rushing to him. It is for him whether he uses that buzzer or does not use it. Who am I to say that he should have his attendant by his side or somebody else? It is for him to decide; he would decide whether his attendant sleeps there or in the adjoining room. I cannot answer all these things.'

Dahyabhai V Patel had his own doubts. 'May I know whether oxygen was available and it was administered, because in such a case, normally oxygen is a thing that gives great relief to a heart patient. Was oxygen administered?'

The minister answered: 'I have been informed that Dr Chugh had arrangements for oxygen and the Health Minister has confirmed that he had all the arrangements for oxygen and everything was done which was required to be done.' Vajpayee was not satisfied with this answer so he cited the press report that said that no oxygen was given. Swaran Singh said he could not say anything more than what was contained in the doctors' report. Another member, MP Bhargava, wanted to know whether there was any truth in the contention that the Russian government wanted 'Shastri to stay with all the other Indian delegates in the same building where they had provided all arrangements for heart specialists to be there all the twenty-four hours?' The minister responded in the negative, saying that, 'the villa in which the Prime Minister stayed had originally been earmarked for him.'

With this short discussion in Parliament, the matter was rested. So it seemed. Then all of a sudden in 1967, it blew up by way of a dirty war between two Mumbai-based tabloids. Their flamboyant Parsi editors accused each other of acting at the behest of the American and Soviet intelligence services. The start was quite innocuous. Pro-Soviet Union investigative weekly *Blitz* ran an obituary for Shastri in its 15 January 1966 edition. Editor Russi Karanjia paid tributes to Shastri's leadership saying that he died at the height of his glory. He recounted that before going to Tashkent Shastri had written him a letter—'his very last message before his final journey'—in which he underlined that India was attending the meeting 'with a firm resolve to succeed and bring lasting peace'. Karanjia commented that the letter dated 2 January, which *Blitz* had originally published in its January edition, was of 'historical significance to the judgment which posterity will be called upon to pass on this splendid little man'. He added that Shastri's 'last letter came to us unsolicited and without any obvious provocation' and that it spoke 'volumes for his passion about peace'.

> What greater glory or finale can any human being ask of God? The nation is bereaved; our people feel orphaned; but Shashtri ji has left the world in a blaze of glory, greater in peace than in war, indeed a martyr to the cause of peace for which he toiled so hard that it took his life. Let Tashkent with its peaceful and fraternal spirit, therefore, be our memorial, as indeed the whole world's memorial,

> to the great little man whose soul has been translated into eternity.

More than a year later, on 25 March 1967, this emotional interpretation of a tragedy was turned into a morbid tale of intrigue by a sensational revelation in *March of the Nation*. This paper was run by Lok Sabha MP Piloo Mody, who was reviled in certain circles in India as a "CIA agent" for he was married to an American and, consequently, was not hostile towards America where he had been educated as well. The *March* story was actually based on an article published on 27 February in Beirut-based Lebanese paper *Az-Zaman* by its diplomatic commentator writing from New Delhi.

The *Az-Zaman* article made three charges. One, Soviet Union had duped India by supplying sub-standard rockets, which failed miserably during the 1965 war. Two, Tashkent summit was a hoax designed to make India and Pakistan unwitting tools of Soviet diplomacy. That is to say, while yielding dividends for Soviet Union, the summit was actually a failure for India, although the Indian government tried to make it look like it was a success. Three, the Shastri letter published in *Blitz* was a fake. Publication of this forged letter was meant to "deceive Indian public opinion into taking a favourble position on the Tashkent accord" and this "served Moscow well" after Shastri died.

March of the Nation asked for an inquiry into the letter affair, commenting that if the document was original, a copy would be available at the Prime Minister's Secretariat (now Prime Minister's Office). It added that if the letter was found to be fraudulent, it would put "an entirely different complexion on the Tashkent affair—and on the Soviet Union's role in pushing the Tashkent Agreement".

Not taking the charge lying down, *Blitz* launched into a blitzkrieg of counter charges peppered with personal slurs against Mody. On 2 July 1967, Karanjia returned the fire with a screaming banner headline: "Hands off *Blitz*, CIA—or you'll get a bloody nose!" Claiming that the Government of India had "no reason to doubt the authenticity of the letter", he characterised *Az-Zaman* as "pro-American". In the 22 July edition, *Blitz* asked "people of India to beware of the invisible hand of the CIA". The following week, Karanjia claimed that "someone (maybe CIA) invented this forgery".

On 5 August, an unrelenting *March* in a front page story detailed what it said were clear signs that the letter was fake. "Since when has the Prime Minister started writing letters without a serial number? ...We know Shastri was a modest man. It is indeed strange to find a letterhead with the Ashoka Crest emanating from the Prime Minister's House... the quality and age of the typewriter used for a letter of such historical importance, which was intended to switch Indian public opinion overnight and pave the way for a successful Tashkent accord". Another story in the same edition, dared both *Blitz* and the Government of India to furnish both the original and the copy of the letter for public scrutiny. "If it does exist, it should be a simple matter to prove it".

As the slanging match continued, *March* on 30 December entered a different level by drawing a "logical inference" that "if the letter is a forgery, then it means that whoever planted it on the *Blitz* must have known there was no real risk of Shastri coming back and repudiating it". *March* insisted it was not suggesting that "the Soviet government, and most assuredly Premier Kosygin, had anything to do with Shastri's death", but KGB sometimes acts "surreptitiously on its own". Without saying in as many words, it linked the Soviet intelligence, or some rogue elements of it, to Shastri's death.

> Finally, it is in the Soviet government's interest to investigate the matter and find out whether some overzealous KGB officials planted the letter on *Blitz* or not and indulged in activities which, for the present, had better remain nameless.

By December 1967, the fake letter controversy had reached Parliament, where, Rajya Sabha member Abid Ali asked the Prime Minister to state 'the result of enquiry conducted by the Government' in view of claims in *Blitz* and *March* and 'what action has been taken by the Government thereon?' Despite the seriousness of the charges, Indira Gandhi incredibly answered that 'no enquiry has been conducted as none was considered necessary.' Taken aback, Ali joined issue with her. 'Is it not a fact,' he asked, that '*Blitz* has claimed that there are huge files having investigation papers in the Defence Ministry, External Affairs Ministry, the Prime Minister's Secretariat, the Information and Broadcasting Ministry and other Government Departments? I never saw a denial on the part of the Government. When such an important issue has been mentioned…'

At this point interruptions marred the House proceeding. After a pause, Ali continued:

> It has also been alleged that the Russian secret society is involved. So far as the Prime Minister of Russia is concerned, he is not involved. I have respect for him. But so far as the KGB is concerned, the counterpart of the CIA, may I know from the Prime Minister whether there has been an enquiry? If there is no enquiry, may I

> know why they do not contemplate an enquiry when it has been mentioned that there has been a forgery?

To this, Indira Gandhi repeated that 'no enquiry was conducted because we did not think that an enquiry was necessary.' She recalled that the matter was brought to her notice earlier by others also, with one lawmaker, UN Trivedi, suggesting that Karanjia 'be asked to produce the original letter for expert scrutiny.' But, Indira Gandhi told Abid Ali, 'this is a matter regarding which I cannot say anything.' She washed her hands off the matter. 'Of course if Shri Karanjia shows the letter to those who doubt its authenticity, it would be a good thing. But it is up to him to consider whether be does that or not.'

The published record of the House proceeding thereafter reads as follows:

> SHRI ABID ALI: Will the Prime Minister be kind enough to ask for this letter at least? My claim is that it is in five pieces, different pieces collected from different places and having been put together. It has been claimed that the letter contains the despatch number. Will it be possible for her to refer to the records and compare whether it has at all been issued?
>
> MR. CHAIRMAN: The Question Hour is over.

On 2 May 1968, Ali again raised the same question in view of a fresh media report, and received the same reply from Gandhi: 'The Government did not consider any enquiry to be necessary.'

This fresh media report had appeared in *Current*, another Mumbai-based weekly, which was edited by a yet another famous Parsi. West-educated DF Karaka started out as a Nehru supporter like Karanjia, but over a period of time turned completely against him and was said to have been put under surveillance. On 6 January 1968, *Current* claimed in an investigative report that the PM's office had actually "searched high and low" for the alleged letter. It quoted a certain Mr Banerjee, a Secretary to the PM, saying that "no copy of this letter exists in the records of the Prime Minister's office". According to the magazine, opposition MPs were not satisfied with the Prime Minister's reply to Ali, the lack of precision on such a serious matter, and were likely to call for a full discussion when Parliament reconvened.

Current opined that in case such a discussion took place it was likely that the KGB would figure in it. "It is learned that there is sufficient consternation in the *Blitz* office and in the Soviet Embassy and its Bombay Consulate, over the concern and the tenacity shown by MPs now even from within the Congress ranks over the part to be played by the KGB in India". *Current* sarcastically commented that "perhaps, if pushed to the wall, *Blitz* is likely to claim that it was planted on him by the American CIA".

Of course, *Blitz* would never do such a thing. There was no further discussion on the alleged Shastri fake letter issue following Indira Gandhi's terse reply in May 1968. But what *Current* had commented in jest was perhaps just as well. Long after everyone had forgotten about the controversy, authentic light was shone on it by the most unlikely person—the man who crafted the forged letter. Walter McIntosh, a former top operative from CIA's Operations Directorate, owned this up in an article he submitted to the CIA for clearance. The agency approved it with so many cuts that there was nothing left worth publishing.

McIntosh then turned to someone who was interested in exploring and writing about such things. Ted Gup is applauded in America for his articles and books on government secrecy, though many disapprove of his revealing in 1992 the existence of a top secret underground bunker to house the Congress of the United States in case of a nuclear attack. With regard to the Shastri fake letter case, McIntosh's reasoning to Gup appears in the latter's 2007 book, *Nation of Secrets: The Threat to Democracy and the American Way of Life*. By this time Piloo Mody and DF Karaka were long dead and *Blitz*, *March*, *Current* had all folded up. At 94, Karanjia was most unlikely to know about certain pages from a book that on the face of it had nothing to do with India. He died in 2008.

McIntosh told Gup that secrecy was fine, but not when it's "just covering up embarrassing things". In his view, if the CIA had proof or suspicions about the KGB assassinating a foreign leader, it needed to be brought out and not covered up "because we are embarrassed because of how we learned of it". With this thought process, McIntosh briefed Gup about the contents of his article the CIA had virtually censored. It was horrifyingly titled—"Did CIA unwittingly assist the KGB in the assassination of India's Prime Minister Shastri?"

The cold war was all about both superpowers increasing their sphere of influence, especially in big countries like India. One reason the Russians got closer to India was because they saw the country as a formidable counterweight to China, which despite being a fellow communist nation, was actually their rival. The article by McIntosh suggested that Shastri was less of a reliable friend of the Soviets than his predecessor Nehru. But when the war between India and Pakistan broke out in 1966, USSR achieved a diplomatic coup by arranging for the conference between the warring nations in Tashkent. This was not something the CIA was pleased with. So, in order to foil the Russian gain, they ran a small operation with a view to driving a wedge between "the independent-minded Shastri and the Soviets".

It was CIA's Technical Services Division that (Gup wrote in his book sourcing the claim to McIntosh), forged the letter and planted it in *Blitz*, using services of an agent of the agency in the weekly. "The idea was that an irate Shastri, upon learning of the note on his return from Tashkent, would denounce it as a fake, disavow its pro-Soviet stance, and further distance himself from Moscow".

The forged letter was deliberately embedded with subtle errors so that it could eventually be revealed as a Communist dirty trick, implicating the Soviets thereby. But things did not quite work out the way the CIA imagined. Gup writes that the CIA learned years later that their man in *Blitz* was "a double agent" who wasted no time in apprising his handler in the KGB of the CIA's scheme.

> And on 11 January 1966, just hours after the Tashkent Conference's successful conclusion, in which a ceasefire and pullback were negotiated, Shastri was found dead in his hotel room. It was said he had had a heart attack,

> but some suspected the Soviets had a hand in his death, desiring a more dependable and less independent prime minister. …As for the letter that the ClA had expected Shastri to denounce upon his return, it would instead resonate as being among the late prime minister's final words. As if to rub the CIA's nose in its failure, *Blitz*, in a tribute to Shastri following his death, ran the same note again in its 15 January issue, along with yet another photo of Shastri between Khan and Kosygin. Under the headline "He Died at the Height of Glory!"[1]

Ted further wrote, suggestively, that Indira Gandhi came to power after Shastri and "proved to be a steadfast friend of Moscow". He described McIntosh's torment of suspecting that the letter crafted by him as a member of the CIA's Technical Services Division back then "played into the Soviets' hands, affording them the perfect opportunity to 'eliminate' Shastri with pro-Soviet sentiments (albeit the CIA's) on his lips and before he could denounce them".

---

1 Ted Gup, **Nation of Secrets: The Threat to Democracy and the American Way of Life**, Anchor; Reprint edition (October 14, 2008).

THREE

Rumble in Rajya Sabha

THE SHASTRI DEATH controversy would have faded away had it not been for the reopening of the Subhas Chandra Bose case in the late 1960s. In Samar Guha, a former freedom fighter and chemistry professor, Netaji's supporters found a formidable one-man army. From the day he took oath as a member of the Lok Sabha in 1963, Guha started hitting the Government and the Congress party. Citing the absence of Netaji's portrait in the Central Hall of Parliament, he charged in his maiden speech that 'it is not an omission but… a deliberate and calculated act on the part of the Congress government.'

By dint of his sheer determination and untiring lobbying efforts, Guha was able to persuade a group of like-minded persons—Atal Bihari Vajpayee and Madhu Limaye being the most prominent—in and out of

Parliament who formed a "national committee". Together, they also sought a fresh inquiry into Netaji's fate. The Government wouldn't relent and Guha wouldn't yield. His opportunity came when in 1966 the Government without wasting much time set up a commission to probe the larger conspiracy behind Mahatma Gandhi's assassination.

As a declassified PMO note shows, 44 MPs wrote to Prime Minister Indira Gandhi seeking an inquiry into the Netaji episode the same way. When the Government still did not agree, Guha lobbied even harder and enlisted support from hundreds of MPs, including those from the Congress party. Eventually, as reported in the *Hindustan Times*, various ministers, in a cabinet meeting, opined that "Government should not have given the impression that it was against a fresh inquiry, when millions of people were interested in knowing what had happened to Netaji", and the refusal to inquire into the matter was creating an "impression among some people that there was something to hide".

So, by 1970, when it was clear that there would be an inquiry commission into the Netaji case, those seeking a probe in the Shastriji matter became active again. Early that year, *Organiser* (the RSS mouthpiece) and *Indian Monitor* provided fresh impetus by publishing stories which called for a proper inquiry into Shastri's death.

The matter resounded in Rajya Sabha when Raj Narain, a veteran of the Quit India movement and maverick politician, sought a response from the Government. When Deputy Chairman of the House, BD Khobragade, did not allow a discussion, TN Singh (a childhood friend of Shastri's, and would-be Chief Minister of UP and later Governor of Bengal) threw his weight behind Narain. 'It is a question about our late Prime Minister, and for some people who were intimately connected with him in his lifetime to be told in a summary fashion that it is not allowed is really not proper,' he said.

Khobragade responded that he understood and appreciated the feelings of the members and if they wanted any discussion, they were 'at liberty to approach the Chairman,' that is the Vice President of India. 'Why should I go?' retorted Singh. He received the backing of Dahyabhai Patel: 'The explanation should be given here. That is the feeling of many people not only in the House but in the whole country.' Khobragade repeated that the MPs 'can approach the Chairman and they can discuss it with him.' At this point, Raj Narain became agitated. He dubbed the Government's attitude as dictatorial.

On 4 March, MPs Lokenath Misra and MK Mohta put a pointed question on the basis of the *Organiser* story. They sought the Government's response to the article claiming "that some unknown factors were responsible for the death of Shri Lal Bahadur Shastri". YB Chavan, now Home Minister, stated that the circumstances of the death were explained by Foreign Minister Swaran Singh in 1966 in the House, and therefore, "there is no justification for any inquiry". This terse response riled the MPs further. They gathered together and in time managed to have a half-hour discussion. This took place on 2 April.

TN Singh opened the discussion. Grieving for his dead friend, he said he felt duty bound to speak out. When Shastri's body arrived, he could not muster courage to see the face. Later in the afternoon, when he caught his last glimpse, he was shocked to see the face discoloured. He developed doubts but could not express them publicly in the hustle of that heartbreaking moment. TN Singh referred to Swaran Singh's statement that PM's suite had a "telephone with a buzzer which could be activated by simply lifting the receiver". He contrasted it with Ram Manohar Lohia's rejoinder in the Lok Sabha that he could not see any telephone in the pictures of Shastri's room. Singh charged the Minister with making a misleading claim.

Singh then questioned Dr Chugh giving Shastri the intra-muscular injection of Mepthentin Sulphate in reclining position. He said he doubted if it was the correct thing to do, adding that he had witnessed his two brothers dying of heart attacks. He asked why Prof Evgenia Yeremenko, the Russian lady doctor who was a witness to Shastri's death along with Dr Chugh, did not sign the medical certificate. Raj Narain alleged at this moment that she had refused to do so.

TN Singh raised his finger of accusation at Mohammed Jan, the cook of Indian Ambassador TN Kaul. 'Where is he? He is neither in Russia and nor in India? He has been transferred to some other country! I have my doubts. I feel sad to be articulating them after having mustered courage to do so. Wherever I went, to villages and towns, people asked me, "What did you do? Why didn't you raise this issue"?'

Speaking for the Government was deputy Home Minister Vidya Charan Shukla, who would attain notoriety during the Emergency as Information and Broadcasting Minister. He began by saying that it would have been better if his senior, Chavan, was there to personally respond as he was in Tashkent during that fateful period. He mollified TN Singh, speaking of his high personal regard for him and stated there might have been lapses but they were not deliberate and there was certainly no intent on the Government's part to cover things up. 'Why would anyone do it?' He clarified that

Mohammed Jan had a clean track record, having worked for Abul Kalam Azad for years. 'He is very much in Delhi and there is no complaint against him.' Shukla spoke politely and offered to do whatever was needed to clear things up. 'Shastriji was a great man of India. Whatever could be done for him was done. If there were mistakes, they were not deliberate. In any case, if need be, we are ready to take proper action,' he submitted. At this, various members, led by Raj Narain, discussed issues related to the lady doctor not signing the death certificate, who gave Shastri the glass of milk, etc. Narain and TN Singh also highlighted that Shastri's personal thermos flask used for keeping milk and water and his personal diary had gone missing. Most importantly, Narain sought from the Government an opportunity to question TN Kaul, Mohammed Jan and other members of Shastri's staff 'so as to arrive at the truth.'

With this, Raj Narain had another surge of emotion. In the heat of the moment, he alleged that Shastri had been killed as a result of a conspiracy and the Government was duty bound to launch an inquiry in order to clear its name. Paying personal compliments to Vidya Charan Shukla, he said he objected to his giving a clean chit to Dr Chugh, who, he further charged, was involved in the 'murder of Dr Lohia.'

In contrast, Mahabir Prasad Bhargava's impassionate

intervention was precise. He said there were certain questions which needed to be 'fairly and squarely replied to by the Government.' His first was, 'Whether it is or it is not a fact that arrangements were made for Shastriji's stay with the Indian Delegation at the hotel and whether all arrangements for a heart patient had been made at that place in a special room constructed and designed for that particular purpose because the Russian government knew that Shastriji was a heart patient?'

His second was, 'Is it or is it not a fact that at the instance of the Ambassador in Russia a telegram was received by the Government of India that Shastriji should not be placed with other members of the Indian delegation and arrangement for him should be made in a particular villa nearabouts the hotel? Where is that blessed telegram which was sent in reply by the Government of India to proceed with the arrangements for Shastriji's stay in that villa separately from the Indian delegation?'

Bhargava, who belonged to the ruling party, queried the Government line buzzer phone. 'My information is that there was no buzzer telephone in that room.'

> The buzzer telephone was in the suite, which has been rightly pointed out by my friend Mr TN Singh in his statement, and anything in this suite cannot be used by

> Shastriji when he was in a particular bedroom. Therefore, a deliberate attempt has been made to mislead this House. That has to be explained by the Government.

He then made a rather serious charge that Russia requested Chavan and Swaran Singh 'to allow post-mortem on Shastriji's body, because they themselves probably suspected some foul play.' That's because, 'they had the honour of their country at the back of their mind and they wanted to be absolutely clear that no foul play was there.'

> Why was his body blue and black? If it is a normal heart attack and death, there is no transformation in the body. It can be explained in two ways. Either some sort of an injection was given to mix up the issue of body turning black and blue, chemically produce some reaction on the body which will make the body become black and blue, and thus, hide the real truth of the body otherwise becoming only blue because of the effect of poison, and thus make it not a natural death. That is another point which has to be explained.

Bhargava ended by saying that over a hundred Members of the Lok Sabha had submitted a memorandum for an inquiry and the 'voice of the Rajya Sabha should join that voice...[in order] to compel the Government to appoint a Commission of Inquiry—a Judicial Commission, headed by a Supreme Court Judge.'

Bhupesh Gupta of the Communist Party of India gave his interpretation at this point. He raised doubts about the veracity of allegations made in *Organiser*. 'This is an RSS journal,' he said. 'I am a little chary of accepting prima facie or even otherwise what is stated in that journal. Certainly it has not approached it from an objective angle. The account that is given in that RSS journal is political. One can see that whenever a Muslim name appears it is in more or less block letters.'

Gupta spoke at length. He said, 'The whole thing is a political build-up. But even then, if there is anything new it should be looked into.' This prompted Raj Narain to tick him off: 'Don't speak with two mouths, Bhupesh!' That started a duel between the two. When discussion resumed, Krishan Kant—who would later be expelled from Congress for his opposition to the Emergency and who became Vice President of India in 1997—opined: 'If it was a matter raised politically by anyone else, I would have opposed it, but when Mr TN Singh raises the question it cannot be a political matter. He raises it from a humanitarian point of view, from a national point of view. I think the honourble Home Minister should study this question and, if necessary, may talk to Mr TN Singh and others who feel about it. He must come before the House and reply to the questions, and if need be, an enquiry should be held. Until an enquiry is held and proper facts are placed before the country, people may not be satisfied on this matter.'

VC Shukla took the floor once more. First he handled the question about who served Shastri the glass of milk. 'Inquiries were made from Ram Nath himself,' he said, 'and he conveyed that it was he who himself served the last glass of milk to Shastriji.' He reiterated that since Chavan himself was present in Tashkent, 'it would be perfectly in order if he could give the benefit of his personal knowledge to this House and to the other House about this matter.' Rajya Sabha Vice Chairman Akbar Ali Khan gave his approval and the Home Minister was requested to make a statement. This happened on 4 April. Chavan's opening remark was that Shastri's death was 'a personal shock' to him and that he 'did not wish to enter into any arguments with my old friends in the House but only place some facts.'

Chavan stated that no security official had ever disapproved of the arrangements for the stay of the Prime Minister in a separate villa as alleged and neither was any telegram sent to Delhi by any of them.

Insisting that Shastri's personal attendant Ram Nath served him the glass of milk and then some water, Chavan decried the impression "that there was something mysterious about Jan Mohammed". There had been no complaint against his character or antecedents, he said. 'He was sent to Tashkent because it was felt that he could be of additional help. His presence was known to our security officers.'

The minister denied charges of inadequacy of the medical arrangements and in particular about the availability of oxygen and the propriety of intra-muscular injections. He cited the response by Minister of Health and Family Planning Dr Sushila Nayar in Lok Sabha that "the physician attending on Shri Shastri did have oxygen also". 'The treatment,' Chavan said, 'should always be left to the attending physician's judgment.'

With regard to Russian doctor Yeremenko not signing the death certificate, Chavan clarified that it was correct to say that she refused to sign the report. 'Since more senior doctors were present and took part in the efforts to revive Shastriji, they signed the report,' he said.

When a member asked what was the point in her alone not signing it when everyone else had, Chavan retorted that 'simply because she did not sign the report, does the whole thing become suspicious?' He denied that the Soviets wanted a post-mortem. 'I may clearly inform the House that no such request was made nor was there any question of declining such a request.'

After several interjections by different MPs, Chavan concluded: 'My impression was and still is that there was nothing suspicious about the death of our dear Prime Minister Lal Bahadur Shastri. As long as I have no suspicion about it, how can I support the demand for enquiry?'

TN Singh and others were still not satisfied. Singh said as long as he lived, he would continue to seek an inquiry.

FOUR

Lalita Shastri opens up

FOR LAL BAHADUR Shastri's shattered widow, the controversy about his death was a never-ending nightmare. The enormity of the tragedy in 1966 had made her, her children, and other close family members numb. Son Anil Shastri, who was then 16, felt he was the most unfortunate. Under the impression that he'd accompany his father and mother to Tashkent, he was sulking when Shastri left. He buried his head in his pillow, refusing to look at his father who had come to say goodbye. Shastri caressed his head and left. When the terrible news came from Tashkent in the dead of night, Anil wept most bitterly.

Now, four years after the tragedy, what with the surge in public demands for an inquiry on one hand and her inability to keep things to herself any longer on the other, Lalita Shastri spoke out. There is another version that this was the first time anyone from the media had approached her. Be that as it may, Lalita Shastri bared her feelings in an interview which appeared in the 4 October 1970 edition of *Dharmyug*, the iconic Hindi weekly, one of the topmost among the mainstream publications in those days. She underlined to her interviewer Prabhat Mittal that TN Kaul had made all the arrangements for Shastriji's stay and Mohammed Jan cooked his meals. Ram Nath served the meals. The narrative that Lalita had reconstructed, having spoken to Shastri's personal staff and information gathered from different sources, was somewhat different from the official version:

> You say that there was something wrong with the milk, but it appears to us that that was not the case. He talked to us on phone some time after taking the milk. It was perhaps fifteen minutes after. Ten or twelve minutes after that he asked for water. There was already a flask kept there with water in it. Ram Nath served water to him out of it. Just a few minutes after taking water, Shastriji told Ram Nath that he should take away the files, papers, etc. and put them in the drawer. He wanted to lie down as he was feeling a sort of heaviness in the head. He sent Ram Nath away to take rest for the night after instructing him to get up early next morning.

As per Lalita Shastri's version published in *Dharmyug* (later excerpted in English in the *Organiser* weekly), unable to speak in his last moments, Shastri had gesticulated that something was wrong with the water he had sipped.

> Shastriji pointed to the flask. Thinking that he wanted water, people present there offered it to him. Shastriji did not take water but he once again pointed in the same direction.

While she thought it was 'not proper to blame Dr Chugh' and neither did she have suspicions about him, Lalita Shastri said 'he was undoubtedly guilty of carelessness' nonetheless. The most shocking part of her statement pertained to the condition of the dead body and attempts made to keep the family members away from it:

> None of us were allowed to go near the body at the airport. Of course I was lost in grief, but Hari tells me that even he had great difficulty in reaching the body. There were blue spots on the body of Shastriji. We were not allowed to go near it even when the dead body was being bathed. It was only after much insistence that we were allowed. Shastriji's face and body had turned blue and were greatly swollen. You will be surprised to

> know that his body was so bloated that the vest had to be torn off it and the kurta could be removed only with difficulty. I did have suspicions at the time but I was in too distressed a state of mind to think about or question it. The surgical mark on the stomach looked like a plus sign. Nobody knows how this came because the medicine for preserving the body was inserted at the back of the neck and there was also a hole there, out of which blood was still oozing. Later on, when some people pointed to the spots on the face someone present quickly brought sandal paste in a small bowl and smeared the whole face with it...but the spots could not be hidden in spite of the sandal coating.

Pictures taken at that time and observations made by others who saw the body substantiate Lalita Shastri's version. Former Delhi Congress chief and Shastriji's follower Jagdish Kodesia was one of those who gave the body the ritualistic bath before it was cremated. In 1990, he wrote the following in a letter to President R Venkatraman:

> We saw a cut at the back of the neck and a cut on the stomach where sticking plaster had been pasted to block the outflow. But the cut at the neck was pouring blood

> and the sheets, pillows and the clothes used by him were all soaked in blood.... We approached the leadership with the request that the body be sent for post-mortem. We were told not to make such a request as this would adversely affect international relations.

Hari Shastri, on 23 November 1970, told the media that his family 'suspected foul play from the very outset' but when he conveyed his suspicions to 'certain Central leaders' soon after his father's body arrived, they asked him 'not to say any such thing at that time'. Lalita Shastri, in her *Dharmyug* interview, underlined another suspicious aspect. Shastri's personal diary and the flask from which he had water before he died had gone missing:

> He always kept it with himself. I don't know whom to blame for its disappearance. What keeps me thinking about this is that Shastriji might have written something for me in it which I will never come to know. The diary and the flask did not come back to us from Tashkent.

In her final assessment, Lalita Shastri felt her husband had been murdered but she was not sure who to blame. She absolved the Russians saying she had no 'doubts about Russia because I think that Shri Kosygin is a very good man. Otherwise also, why any country will kill the leader of another friendly country after inviting him there.' Kosygin had made sure to visit Lalita Shatri to express his personal grief in 1966 and arranged for her visit to Tashkent a few months later.

Lalita Shastri's interview rattled both Indian and the Russian governments. The Russian ambassador, Nikolai Pegov, reportedly protested to the Ministry of External Affairs, castigating what he called 'the efforts of political parties to involve his country in Lal Bahadur Shastri's death in Tashkent.' As reported in *Current* on 20 November, broadcasts on Soviet radios were all fire and brimstone. They denounced the "reprehensible and dirty" demand to inquire into Shastri's death as "ill-motivated and foreign sponsored". Referring to Lalita Shastri's interview, they said that a suspicion was sought to be created that some prominent people in Congress and the supporters of Mrs Gandhi were guilty of the crime.

Dubbing the demand for an investigation as an "election stunt", a broadcast alleged that the United States was behind this dirty game. The Americans and their agents in India had become shaky over the growing friendship between the peoples of the Soviet Union and India and the manner in which India was coming closer to the Soviet Union. Indira Gandhi was advised not to "yield to the pressure from these reactionaries and order for a probe". Stating that setting up an inquiry would "amount to suspecting the Soviet Government and the people", a warning was issued that such a "move would strike at the very roots of friendship between the two countries". In true Soviet fashion, it was added that "Soviet people and the government will not take such an insult lying down and the sole responsibility would be of the Government of India".

In the meanwhile, Lalita Shastri's revelations had prompted the setting up of a national committee to press for the demand for an inquiry into the PM's demise. Comprising lawmakers and notables in public life, it was headed by Dr Hridya Nath Kunzru, freedom fighter and veteran Parliamentarian. The members were: TN Singh, Acharya Kripalani, Suchitra Kripalani, Mahavir Tyagi, HV Kamath, Nath Pai, MC Chagla, AB Vajpayee, Prakash Vir Shastri, Rao P Kondana, AD Mani, KL Gupta, MP Bhargava, MP Das, Raj Narain, BP Mandal, Ram Sewak Yadav, LK Advani, SD Mishra, BN Mandal, DV Gundappa, HS Gurupadaswamy, DL Sengupta , Jagdish Kodesia and Dahyabhai Patel.

The secretary of the committee was Dharam Yash Dev, a multifaceted personality—freedom fighter, diplomat and one of most well known investigative journalists of his time. In several of his incisive articles published in 1970, Dharam Yash Dev tried to poke holes in the official version of the PM's death. On 16 May, he wrote in *Indian Monitor* that:

> According to experts in forensic jurisprudence, an abdominal incision like the one found on Shastriji's body is generally made for the purpose of autopsy or post-mortem and for examining the stomach contents or "stomach wash" as it is commonly described. If the abdominal incision on Shastriji's body was made for this purpose, then it raises a few further but still more pertinent questions:
>
> - What was the "provocation" for the Russians to perform such an autopsy;
> - If they had any good reasons or "doubts" for performing an autopsy—what were these reasons; and
> - What were the findings as a result of this post-mortem or autopsy?
> - Whether these results were made known to the Indian doctor (Dr Chugh) and/or any other members of the Indian delegation, including Ambassador Kaul, who were with Shastriji in Tashkent?

By the end of 1970, Dahyabhai V Patel had published a booklet titled *Was Shastri Murdered?*[1] When suspicions about foul play at Tashkent had initially been voiced, Patel recalled, they were disregarded as springing from fevered imaginations or being motivated by plain malice. He rightly observed that when public figures die there are usually "plenty of sensation-mongers eager to jump to the most morbid conclusions". In most such cases the "inexplicable" is soon explained away and the doubters are laughed to scorn. But in the case of Shastri, Patel emphasised, "exactly the reverse has happened". At first only a very few questioned the official account, "but in the five years…the chorus of doubt has swelled and demands for a top-level inquiry are today being voiced on every side in the press, by Members of Parliament, and by public personages who can, by no stretch of imagination be dubbed irresponsible or prone to morbid fancies". Several puzzling pieces have come to light, he added, that simply refuse to fit neatly into the jigsaw. "It is worth noting that some of these discrepancies and doubts were

---

1 Published by Society for Parliamentary Studies, New Delhi, **Was Shastri Murdered?** went out of circulation long ago. My attempts to locate a copy in various libraries, including the National Library in Kolkata (the largest library in India by volume) and the Central Reference Library in New Delhi's Shastri Bhawan did not succeed. Luckily, a professor friend of mine in a major American university was able to locate a copy in his country for me.

there from the very start and that from the first there have been questions raised that nobody has cared or dared to answer to this day".

Patel gave the example of Moscow Radio's announcement that "at about 01.20 hours on 11 January, Messrs Sahai, Kapur and Sharma told the Prime Minister's doctor (Dr RN Chugh), who was in the next room, that LB Shastri was not feeling well. Dr RN Chugh immediately went to the Prime Minister, who was sitting in his bed coughing, complaining of a lack of air, holding his hands to his chest and looking pale". Patel underlined that Moscow Radio news made "no mention of Shastri having had to stagger to the next room to summon help". According to the Russian broadcast, when Dr Evgenia Yeremenko arrived at Dr Chugh's request, "she found Prime Minister Lal Bahadur Shastri dead". Yet, Patel wrote, "it has been stated in Parliament and in Indian newspapers on several occasions that Dr Yeremenko came while Lal Bahadur Shastri was still alive, and these reports have not been contradicted". He also wondered why "her name does not figure in the version of death report which was presented to Parliament by Mr Swaran Singh" when she was "the first to arrive on the scene".

Was Shastri Murdered? carried the text of an article of Dharam Yash Dev titled "Mystery of two medical reports" published in *Organiser* on 7 November 1970. It referred to the English version of the report about Shastri's death which was tabled in Parliament on 16 February 1966, and another one that was included in a booklet titled *Soviet Union shares India's grief* released by the USSR embassy in New Delhi on 14 January 1966. This report differed with the report tabled in Parliament in certain respects.

- It bore names of eight Soviet doctors; whereas the report made public by Indian government contained six.
- The report tabled in Parliament stated that "it can be considered that the death occurred because of acute attack of infarkt miokarda"; whereas the one released by the embassy stated that "it may be considered that the death was caused by repeated myocardial infraction". Dev commented: 'There is a great deal of difference between the words "it can be considered" and "it may be considered".'

Making out 'a strong case for the KGB being the culprit,' Patel opined that 'the best and cleanest course in the circumstances would be to set up an inquiry commission as soon as possible. The Government's self-righteous assumption that the rest of India must accept Shastri's death as natural because Government has declared it to be so is preposterous. Nobody will take the Government's unsupported word in this matter. Not at this stage when a mass of unrelated evidence all points in the direction of foul play.'

Patel read in attempts by both Indian and Soviet governments 'to block a probe' a clear sign that 'there is something very ugly about the Shastri affair that both Delhi and Moscow are determined to conceal at any cost.'

FIVE

A statement of "facts"

PUSHED TO THE wall by rising public anger in the wake of Lalita Shastri's *Dharmyug* interview, the Government of India towards the end of 1970 was compelled to make a somewhat detailed statement about the tragedy in Tashkent. The trigger was JP Yadav, Gurcharan Singh Tohra, Thillai Villalan, Chitta Basu and Inder Singh raising the issue in Rajya Sabha on 3 December 1970. They asked what steps the Government was going to take. Deputy Home Minister KC Pant said the Government had 'no information beyond what is contained in the press report of a recent interview with Shrimati Lalita Shastri' but was, at the same time, in the process of releasing certain "facts" to the people. This eventually happened on 18 December 1970 when "a statement of facts relating to the death of Lal Bahadur Shastri" was tabled in both

Houses of Parliament.

The statement addressed just about all the charges levelled against the Government, offering seemingly convincing explanations for the lacunae cited by the lawmakers previously. The 18-point statement was bolstered by an annexure containing a copy of the doctors' certificate issued in 1966 along with its official translation, and further clarifications issued by Soviet doctors in November 1970, in view of charges of foul play in India.

At the very start, the statement underlined that Shastri's personal staff comprised people who were singularly devoted to him:

> Dr RN Chugh had been Personal Physician to Shri Shastri since 1955, except for a period of one year, 1959-60, when Dr Chugh was on training abroad. He regularly examined Shri Shastri, generally kept a watch over his health and accompanied him on all tours. While in Delhi he used to secure additional consultation from competent doctors on Shri Shastri's health. Shri Shastri was thoroughly examined on 31 December 1965, and was found in good health. Dr Chugh took to Tashkent the medicines necessary to deal with any acute medical emergency, including equipment for the immediate administration of oxygen. Shri Ram Nath had been

> working with Shri Shastri's family for more than 20 years. All Shri Shastri's personal belongings were in his charge. In Tashkent his duty was to look after all personal needs of Shri Shastri and to remain available to him at all times. He also used to work in the kitchen to help in the preparation of Shri Shastri's food. Shri R Kapur was responsible for the Prime Minister's security. As usual, on tours, he took two flasks for water for the Prime Minister.

The statement clarified the reasons why Shastri was put up in the dacha.

> The villa was about 250 yards from the Intourist Hotel where other members of the Indian Delegation were lodged. It has been alleged that Shri Shastri was originally to stay in the Intourist Hotel but that it was later decided to lodge him at the villa. As was explained by the Foreign Minister in February 1966 in the Rajya Sabha, it is not correct to say that the Prime Minister was first allotted accommodation at the Intourist Hotel and then shifted to the villa. Arrangements were made for Shri Shastri's stay in a separate villa in Tashkent because at the villa—
>
> - he would not have to climb a flight of stairs as he would have to in the Intourist Hotel where suitable

accommodation was available only on the first floor and there was no lift;

- his personal medical and security staff could stay with him, while in the Intourist Hotel they would have had to be accommodated on a different floor;
- he could have separate arrangements for entertaining and meeting guests, while in the Intourist Hotel only a common dining room was available for the entire delegation; and
- it was considered appropriate that the Indian Prime Minister should also have a separate residence as arranged for the leaders of the Pakistan and Soviet delegations.

The Government accepted that there was no bell or phone in Shastri's room, but in the middle of the study adjoining his room, not more than 4 to 5 metres away from his bed, were three phones. The third black colour phone had a buzzer which could be activated simply by lifting the receiver. This was connected with the room occupied by the Medical Officer and the Security Officer. Shastri had been told how to use it and he had used it more than once during his stay.

The necessary security arrangements for the PM at the villa had been made by the Soviet government. The statement read that these arrangements "were checked by the Prime Minister's security staff and were found to be entirely satisfactory".

Regarding Mohammed Jan, the following was stated:

> In addition to the Soviet cooks in the kitchen, there was Shri Mohammed Jan, the cook of the Indian Ambassador in Moscow. Shri Mohammed Jan had for many years before Partition worked with high government officials. For about 11 years, from 1946, he worked as cook for the late Maulana Abul Kalam Azad. After Maulana Azad's death he worked for three years as cook for the Indian High Commissioner in Nairobi, Shri IJ Bahadur Singh. He had been the head cook in the Indian Embassy in Moscow. During all these years of his association with highly placed persons nothing had come to notice which could create the slightest doubt about his trustworthiness. Even after Shri Shastri's death, Shri Mohammed Jan continued to work with our Ambassador in Moscow until the end of 1966. He later worked for about three years as the cook of our Ambassador in Rome. Since October 1969, he has been working at the Rashtrapati Bhavan and no complaint whatsoever against him has come to notice.

The Government underlined that it was Ram Nath

who "brought the food that had been prepared by Shri Mohammed Jan and others in the kitchen, according to the menu indicated by Shri Ram Nath". It was reiterated that it was Ram Nath who gave Shastri some milk with Isabgol late in the night and that "the milk was boiled in the kitchen by Shri Ram Nath himself". It was he who after a while gave some water to Shastri from the flask kept in his bedroom.

> Shri Ram Nath stayed in the Prime Minister's suite till about 12.30 am (Tashkent time) when Shri Shastri asked him to go and have his food. Shri Ram Nath put out the lights and left the Prime Minister's suite. Shri Shastri had until then looked perfectly well and normal and had not complained of any discomfort.

Since questions had been raised about the death certificate—in whose custody it was—why there were differences in Russian and English versions, etc.—the Government cleared the air.

> The medical report was prepared in Russian. It bears the signatures of Dr RN Chugh and 8 Soviet doctors, including the Deputy Minister of Health of the Uzbek Soviet Socialist Republic and Dr Yeremenko. The report

was translated into English by an Indian interpreter. The English translation also was signed by Dr Chugh and six Soviet doctors, including the Deputy Minister of Health of the Uzbek Soviet Socialist Republic. The report in English was handed over to the Indian officers on the spot and has been in the possession of the Ministry of Home Affairs. The photostat copy of the medical report in Russian was obtained from the Soviet authorities in July 1970. On 14 January 1966, *The Soviet Review*, published by the Soviet Embassy in New Delhi, had brought out a supplement on Shri Shastri's death and had included a medical report, in English, showing the signatures of Dr Chugh and 8 Soviet doctors including Dr Yeremenko. This report was clearly an English translation of the medical report in Russian.

There is no difference in the substance of the medical reports drawn up in Russian and in English. However, attention has been drawn to two small differences between them. The first is that while the medical report in English bears the signatures of Dr Chugh and six Soviet doctors, the report in Russian bears the signatures of Dr Chugh and eight Soviet doctors. The report was first drawn up in Russian and Dr Chugh and eight Soviet doctors signed it. The report was translated into English and as it happened only six of the Soviet doctors signed it. The important fact is that both reports were signed on the spot and it would be wholly unreasonable to entertain any suspicion about the authenticity of either. When the matter was discussed in Parliament, some Members had referred to the absence of the signature of Dr EG Yeremenko who had been the first Russian doctor to arrive at the villa. It will be seen that she had signed the medical report in Russian.

The charge that medical reports in Russian and English referred to two different medicines administered to Shastri in his last moments was fairly responded to as well.

The second difference pointed out is that while it is stated in the medical report in Russian that the mixture injected into Shri Shastri's body by the anti-shock group of doctors was of calcium chloride, adrenalin and glucose, the report in English states that it was potassium chloride, adrenalin and glucose. It has been verified from the Soviet authorities that the mixture used was of calcium chloride with adrenalin and glucose. The difference in the two reports obviously is due to a mistake in the translation. The Russian words for calcium and potassium are very similar. They are "kali" for potassium and "kai tsi" for calcium. The Indian translator while translating the Russian report appears to have wrongly translated kaltsi as Potassium (instead of calcium). As the anti-shock treatment had been carried out by the Russian doctors, at the time of signing the report Dr Chugh was not in a position to locate this mistake. It will be also appreciated that the discrepancy between the two medical reports relates to a drug which was injected after Shri Shastri's death as a part of the anti-shock reanimation treatment. By no reasoning can this discrepancy be construed as creating a suspicion about the cause of Shri Shastri's death.

The official statement then came to responding to the charges that there were cut marks on Shastri's body and the reason why there were blue spots on it.

After the reanimation treatment had been given up, Shri Shastri's body was embalmed by the Soviet doctors, in the presence of Dr RN Chugh to check quick decomposition. The embalming liquid consisting of three litres of pure spirit, one litre of formalin and 200 grams of urotropine was introduced through an incision into the femoral

> artery in the inguinal[1] part of the body. The incision was covered by plaster-tape. No other incision was made on Shri Shastri's body and no part of the body was taken out for examination or for any other purpose. Some change of colour of the body of Shri Shastri was quite natural, since such phenomenon does occur consequent to embalming.

According to the statement, as per the clarification issued by Soviet doctors in November 1970, "they had not given any injection or made any incision in the area of the neck on the body of Shri Shastri and have said that they had not noticed any bleeding wound in the area of the neck". It was also stated that "the members of the Indian delegation and the Prime Minister's personal staff also did not notice any such wound". Soviet doctors had issued the clarification in response to "fabrications" in Indian newspapers about Shastri's death. They stated that the Health Ministry of the Uzbek Republic had set up "medical aid posts with qualified Soviet doctors in attendance 24 hours a day" in the immediate vicinity of the dacha where Shastri was lodged. "The necessary modern medical equipment and medical supplies were

1 "Inguinal" relates to the region of the groin or the lower lateral regions of the abdomen.

available at these posts".

With regard to Shastri's belongings, the statement said that an inventory of all the baggage of Shastri, including his personal effects, was made. Those personal effects were packed by Ram Nath. Every cupboard and drawer in the suite in the Tashkent dacha was searched "to make sure that nothing was left behind". The case containing two thermos flasks "was brought back by the Security Officer". The statement asserted that "there was no diary" in Shastri's personal effects, and "nobody saw a diary with him in Tashkent". On arrival in New Delhi the inventory of the personal baggage was again checked and "the tally of the articles was found to be correct".

Lastly, the statement tackled the point whether it was not a fact that a close relation of Shastri had suggested to the acting Prime Minister, Gulzari Lal Nanda, that there should be a post-mortem examination of Shastri's body. "There is no record of any such suggestion having been made" the statement said, adding that "Shri Nanda has stated that he has no recollection of anyone having spoken to him about a post-mortem examination".

But in spite of this statement, the Opposition members were not satisfied. In the Rajya Sabha in particular, there followed a debate which turned nasty at times. Opening it was LK Advani. He made a point of order questioning the procedure adopted by the Government. Advani said the MPs were seeking a statement from the Government since the beginning of the session of Parliament. 'I asked the Minister myself last week and he told me they were almost ready with the statement. Now we find that on the very last day of this session the statement is being made.'

> ...in this particular case the timing is deliberate, it is mala fide and is intended to deprive this House of an opportunity to debate this important question. ...this sort of conduct on the part of the Government should invite strictures from the Chair....

This was followed by a heated exchange of words between the Deputy Chairman of the House and members, especially Raj Narain. Consequently, the House was adjourned. When it met again fifteen minutes past three, Raj Narain also expressed his annoyance that such a statement was made on the last day of the session. He stated that he was the first person to raise the matter of Shastri's death in Rajya Sabha, and late Ram Manohar Lohia in Lok Sabha. Both held the view that Shastri was murdered. He repeated his charge that there was a "conspiracy" behind Shastri's death, which was "not natural". He claimed that on 14 December itself the "national committee" led by Hridya Nath Kunzru had come to know of the Government's tactics to place the statement in the House on the last day of the session to deprive the members of a full-fledged discussion on it.

'Will this not raise doubts?'he asked. 'It will. These tactics adopted by the Government will convey the message in every nook and corner of the country that the Government doesn't want proper light on the reasons behind Shastri's death.' Raj Narain reasoned that the MPs should have been given enough time so that they could study the statement properly and then frame questions. Amid verbal clashes with members who were with the Government, Raj Narain continued to make one allegation after another. He said Shastri was India's first "Indian" Prime Minister, as before him India had an English Prime Minister (Nehru). Shastri was born in a poor household and yet became PM. He alleged that there were people who wanted to become Prime Minister and wanted Shastri to die. 'Shastri was killed and this government did not set up a committee to inquire into it,' he alleged. Dahyabhai Patel backed Raj Narain saying that he too had been pressing the Rajya Sabha Chairman 'to tell the Government to make a statement for the last one week' as he had suspicions about the Government's intentions. 'My suspicions have been fully borne out.'

Amid disruptions, the debate continued, revolving around the procedural issues, whether or not Rajya Sabha should extend its session in order to have a detailed discussion. This was opposed by Congress MPs. 'We do not want to continue this House tomorrow,' said Purabi Mukhopadhyay. 'We have all fixed up our appointments from Monday. So, Sir, today being the last day, let us adhere to the business of the day.'

Raj Narain was riled by such statements and by what he thought was the partisan role played by the chair. He again started blasting the Government, alleging that Shastri's attendant Ram Nath was under pressure from government to stick to the official version. 'He is being induced as well as threatened. Where is Shastri's thermos and personal diary?' He charged that there was no reason for Shastri's body to decompose as it was brought to India within hours of death. He alleged that post-mortem was not carried out because he was poisoned and that's why the Government kept people in the dark.

After some more acrimonious moments, Pitambar Das spoke about an anomaly he had noticed in the medical report in Russian and its English translation. He read out the portion of the statement where it said that "the report was first drawn up in Russian and Dr Chugh and 8 Soviet doctors signed it. The report was translated into English and as it happened only 6 of the Soviet doctors signed it".

> But you will see that of these six doctors, one is that doctor who has not signed the Russian report at all. How did he come in?

Das's interpretation was that "any one of these documents, or both of them, have been forged". He asked the Government to explain this, stating that 'only an enquiry into the whole affair can explain this thing.' Ram Niwas Mirdha, the Minister of State in the Ministry of Home Affairs, responded: 'When I read paragraph 10, I myself said that one report bears the signature of Dr Chugh and eight Soviet Doctors, and the English translation bears the signature of Dr Chugh and six Soviet doctors.' Das interjected to say, 'The explanation that you give is that the report was first drawn up in Russian and Dr Chug and 8 Soviet doctors signed it. It is all right. The report was translated into English and, as it happened only 6 of the Soviet doctors signed it. It means only 6 out of those 8 signed it. If you look at the report in English there is the signature of Dr YY Gordon. This signature does not appear on the Russian report. How did it happen? ... Why was the new doctor brought?' Mirdha responded that the Government had no desire to hide anything and accused that some MPs were distorting facts and seeing "ghosts which are not there".

A verbal squabble ensued between Pitambar Das and Ram Niwas Mirdha. Addressing the Deputy Chairman of the House, Mirdha said, 'Sir, there are two lists, Russian and English. And I would repeat that the name of Dr Gordon appears in both these lists. The signature is there in both the lists.'

Das would not concede: 'On what number is it? I ask this question because number three is not in the English list, number 8 is not there and number 9 also is not there. Similarly, you can tell me which number is Gordon in the Russian list?'

'The first seven signatures that appear in the Russian list are also there in the English list.'

'No. Which is Gordon's?'

Now more MPs joined the debate. Mahavir Tyagi exhorted Mirdha to, 'read out the names of the signatures in the Russian list.' Sundar Singh Bhandari asked, 'What is the serial number of Gordon in the Russian list?' When Mridha parroted that 'there are seven names that appear in both the lists and the third signature in the English as well as the Russian list is that of Gordon,' Das asked the Deputy Chairman to compare the lists. The Deputy Chairman then said:

> Pitamber Das has tried to make out that the third signature on both the reports is not the same. But if we see the Russian report—it is a photostat copy—just in front of the signature, the name of Mr Gordon is written. I do not think there can be any difference between the name and the signature. Had there been any difference between the signature and the name, that would have been a very glaring mistake on the face of the document and I do not think anybody would commit such a glaring mistake on the face of the record. That is one thing. Secondly, on the Russian report the signature of Dr Gordon is not so clear. But, of course, I am not a handwriting expert. When you refer to the "don" in the Russian as well as the English reports you will find that there is some similarity between the last letters "don" in both the reports. From these it appears that the signature on both the reports is of the same person. That is what I feel. I am not a handwriting expert.

'It is only a matter of opinion,' Das shot back. 'You can say that,' the Deputy Chairman said, 'But I do not think the honourable Minister would take that much risk to say that these are the signatures of Dr Gordon when they were not...' Das replied: 'Mr Deputy Chairman, you have said that the Minister would not take the risk of saying that they are the signatures of Dr Gordon if they were really not. I could have accepted it, provided this statement was made outside the House because in that case, I could have proceeded against him in a Court of Law.'

'You can proceed against him in this House also for breach of privilege,' the Deputy Chairman retorted.

LK Advani returned to the discussion. Pointing out that the Government's statement itself agreed that there was a mistake in mentioning the right name of the medicine administrated to Shastri in his last moments, he observed that 'this in itself is something very serious,' considering it involved the death of the Prime Minister. 'The Government has come out with this kind of callous report and is trying to justify or whitewash everything.' He questioned why the Government all the while remained silent when lawmakers said there were incision marks on Shastri's body. 'Why was this not told to this House or the other House at an earlier stage? It is only when the matter has been raised in the papers and the press and the *Dharamyug* that they have come out with this kind of statement. The suspicion of the people that fair play has not been done and justice has not been done is fully justified and the whole thing is sought to be covered and white-washed.'

From this point on, the discussion started to

disintegrate into recriminations. Members levelled charges against each other. Notably, Vidyawati Chaturvedi (Congress) alleged that TN Singh had raised the issue for political reasons as he was silent when he was part of the Central government. Chandra Shekhar, the would be Prime Minister, who was then firmly with Indira Gandhi, claimed that the matter was being raised as a smokescreen to obfuscate other ongoing issues. Raj Narain single-handedly kept on crossing swords with others. He was speaking when the Deputy Chairman said that with the lawmakers squabbling among themselves he had no option but to adjourn the House sine die.

In the Lower House, Minister of State for Home Affairs, KC Pant, laid on the Table the same statement. The first MP to speak was Dr Ram Subhag Singh from Buxur. He objected to the statement being made public on the last day of the session of Parliament. Atal Bihari Vajpayee, by then a Lok Sabha MP, echoed this view. Senior parliamentarian, Prakash Vir Shastri, said he too had issued repeated cautions that the Government was out to stifle a proper discussion on the matter by tabling its statement on the last day of the session. He said Shastri's death was a mystery, and tabling of the statement on the last day of the session was another mystery. He sought to clarify from the minister whether or not it was true that prior to Shastri's visit to Tashkent, a security officer, GC Dutta, had been to the city and sent a cable to New Delhi expressing dissatisfaction with the arrangements of Shastri's stay made by Ambassador TN Kaul. Prakash Vir Shastri wondered whether the Government was going to make those cables of Dutta public.

GC Dutta's name had figured earlier as well. Without mentioning his name and that of Mohammed Jan, Dharam Yash Dev had made serious allegations in an article in *Economic and Political Weekly*. He claimed that "the shift from the Intourist Hotel to the Villa was a last minute brainwave of our Ambassador in Moscow, against the advice of the top Security men who had earlier visited Tashkent to check on the arrangements made for the Indian Prime Minister's stay".

> An "outsider" without proper security clearance was "planted" at the Villa, ostensibly to assist Shri Shastri's old personal servant who had gone with him all the way from India to look after the Prime Minister with regard to his food and other personal comforts. This "outsider" was a personal bearer of our Ambassador in Moscow who was specially brought to Tashkent, even though there were no good reasons for him to be present there.

On 11 August 1967, in the Rajya Sabha, Mahabir Prasad Bhargava posed the same question as Prakash Vir Shastri. On behalf of the Ministry of Home Affairs, Vidya Charan Shukla gave a written answer, which merely said "no". This wasn't, in my view, an adequate response. Much of what Bhargava said about the Shastriji death matter had a ring of credibility around it. His observations were logical and incisive. GC Dutta, I gather from books and a journal published long afterwards[2], was PM's security-in charge, a Joint Director in the Intelligence Bureau. He remained in that position after Indira Gandhi became Prime Minister.

Unlike in the Rajya Sabha, the discussion in the Lok Sabha on 18 December 1970 did not last long. Following the lead of Prakash Vir Shastri, many lawmakers tried to have a structured discussion. But Speaker Gurdial Singh Dhillon wouldn't allow it. 'You can ask questions about delay and other things, but if you want to go into the detailed discussion of the merits, that can be taken up only during a regular debating hour,' he said. Shiv Narayan of Basti objected. He said this was a matter of India's prestige, involving the death of a prime minister and warranted

2 GC Dutta's name appears in recent publications, such as **The Indian Police Journal** (October-December, 2012, Special Issue) and 2009 book **Train to India: Memories of Another Bengal** by former IB Joint Director Maloy Krishna Dhar.

an inquiry. The Speaker ticked him off, saying he was an experienced member and should have raised matter related to procedures. Prakash Vir Shastri intervened to say that he merely wanted some clarifications for which he wanted the Speaker's approval. The Speaker, however, said: 'It is a question between the members and the Government to ask for the debate. I am concerned with the procedure to be followed.' This led to an uproar among the MPs. 'I think I will need a number of aspirins today. It is a regular headache for me,' the Speaker said.

Prakash Vir Shastri implored Gurdial Singh Dhillon not to treat the matter as ordinary. But Dhillon was firm. 'I thought you will raise some procedural or technical objections. I did not allow you to have a regular debate on this. I am very sorry.' This prompted Prakash Vir Shastri to remark that Dhillon was 'trying to save some people' by becoming an accomplice in what the Government was doing to conceal the facts about Prime Minister Shastri's death. The final answer of the Speaker which ended the discussion was: 'I am not allowing you more time.'

This is how, by the end of 1970, the Shastri death controversy became dormant. The general elections in March 1971 followed by the war with Pakistan heralded India into a new era where there was little space for the legacy of Shastri, what to speak of his death. His widow quietly passed her days never able to reconcile with the official position. Driven by despair, Lalita Shastri once even took an occultist route to try and find out about the "murder" in Tashkent. She went to see one Gauri Shankar Sahai, who supposedly enabled her to communicate with the spirit of her husband.

SIX
Case revisited

LONG AFTER IT was consigned to the domain of conspiracy theories, the Shastri death matter was briefly revisited in the 1980s and beyond by top government officials present in Tashkent on that fateful day. Having retired long ago, they now felt free to give their personal takes through their books. Ironically though, the man who knew the best, kept more or less mum despite being the most prolific writer among these former top officials.

As he was heralded into the Oval office to meet President Gerald Ford as India's Ambassador in 1974, handsome and swashbuckling Triloki Nath Kaul was introduced by US Secretary of State Henry Kissinger as someone who had been 'in every important post in India's Foreign Service—Moscow, Peking, Washington.' TN Kaul was also Foreign Secretary from 1967 -1972. The

Americans regarded him as pro-Russia, which was no great secret. In 2013, Kaul's birth centenary was celebrated at Russian Cultural Centre in New Delhi in the presence of Indian foreign minister and Russian ambassador. When Kaul was appointed as India's ambassador to the US in 1973, then US ambassador Daniel Patrick Moynihan sent a cable to Washington DC, whose text was divulged in 2013 by WikiLeaks. Moynihan's description was not very flattering:

> Kaul, like Nehru family, is a Kashmiri Brahmin, self-assured to the point of arrogance by birth. His career, as ambassador to Moscow and recently as foreign secretary, has been marked by pro-Soviet bias and concomitant anti-American words and deeds.

Moynihan stated he had not met Kaul but gathered that he was 'inclined toward slyness, especially in his dealings with Westerners.'

Reminiscences, discreet and indiscreet (Lancers Publishers, New Delhi) by TN Kaul was published in 1982. Living up to its title, this fascinating book indeed had many frank recollections. In a sensational one, Kaul recalled that in 1962 when he was the deputy High Commissioner of India in the UK, Morarji Desai visited

London. "Fed up with Desai's pretence and fads", Kaul took Desai (a staunch follower of Mahatma Gandhi), and High Commissioner MC Chagla (a former judge and Central minister) to watch a play. During the play, two beautiful actresses moved into the audience and made themselves comfortable in the laps of Indian dignitaries. Chagla chuckled when Kaul told it was he who had set up this prank. He told Kaul that he enjoyed the joke and 'Desai really loved it, though he pretended not to".

If only Kaul had been as forthcoming as this with regard to the Tashkent mishap in his book. But all that he would write was that Shastri had a "sad and untimely demise". That's all. So much for his reminiscences, discreet and indiscreet!

In 1983 was released *From Bandung to Tashkent: Glimpses of India's Foreign Policy* (Sangam Books) by CS Jha, who was India's Foreign Secretary in January 1966 and, like Kaul, present in Taskhent. This book was better than Kaul's recollections in the respect that it devoted a few paragraphs to Shastri's death. Jha described what had happened that night, how he came to know of Shastri's sudden illness. He wrote that he might have had "a vague premonition of the coming catastrophe" as he was not able to sleep that night before he was given the bad news. Jha narrated how Shastri's body was taken to the airport and then to Delhi. "The poignancy and the solemnity of the tragic scene are forever engraved in my memory".

Jha went on to theorise in a short paragraph that emotional and physical strain of the Tashkent summit might have caused Shastri's death. He stated that going back on his public commitment in India of not withdrawing from Haji Pir Pass and other strategic areas troubled Shastri a lot. He referred to the 10-11 January midnight telephonic talk Shastri had with his son or son-in-law during the course of which he was told that the Tashkent declaration had evoked strong criticism in India. "A combination of all these factors could have snapped the life of even a healthier man than Shastri", Jha concluded, making no other reference to the controversy.

In the 1990s two more accounts became available. They came from bureaucrats who were Shastriji's admirers, though about one of them the members of Shastri's family have a different view. LP Singh, who was Home Secretary in January 1966, published a biography of Shastri in 1996. In *Portrait of Lal Bahadur Shastri: A Quintessential Gandhian* (Ravi Dayal Publisher), Singh drew a clear conclusion that Shastri's death was natural; there was nothing mysterious about it in view of his medical history. At the same time, he refuted the version that Shastri "had broken down under stress", pressing that he was not of an infirm character. The statement made in Parliament in December 1970, Singh claimed, left no doubt in anyone's mind, but "some in India needlessly look for conspiracy theories to explain major occurrences".

After returning to Delhi from Tashkent, LP Singh consulted top cardiologist Dr MM Singh, a Harvard Medical School graduate who become Chief of Medicine at New York State University. Dr Singh said Shastri evidently suffered from acute myocardial infarction "from which he would have died even if he were already in an oxygen tent in an American hospital". Dr Singh observed nothing suspicions in the chain of events as narrated to him, dismissing charges of Russians not giving him prompt medical aid.

The second and by far the most detailed account of Prime Minister Shastri's death was rendered by Sir CP Srivastava in his 1996 book *Lal Bahadur Shastri: A life of truth in politics* (Oxford University Press). Srivastava, the Joint Secretary to PM Shastri, was an outstanding person who received Padma Bhushan and Padma Vibhushan in 1972 and 2009. He also excelled as the Secretary-General of the London-based UN International Maritime Organization for four successive terms, during which time he was knighted by the British monarch. But countless knew him as the husband of Nirmala Srivastava, founder of Sahaja Yoga movement that has adherents all over the world.

Srivastava wrote in his well-received book that Shastri probably was not very careful about his health. He worked long hours without taking rest. Because he was not present at the moment of the Prime Minister's death in the dacha, Srivastava relied on the accounts of Jagannath Sahai and MMN Sharma to piece together a vivid account of Shastri's last moments. Emphasizing that they were "loyal and devoted to Shastri", Srivastava wrote that having known the two for years he had "full confidence in the truthfulness and accuracy of their accounts". In view of the charges of poisoning, which allegedly led to Shastri's body turning bluish, Srivastava first questioned the aides and was told by Sahai that he had been informed by Dr Chugh that this was due to embalming. In all fairness, Srivastava had the details provided by Shastri's personal aides along with medical certificates of 1966 and 1970 issued by the Soviets run through reputed British forensic pathologist Iain West.

Dr West opined that cyanosis (discolouration of the skin) was quite consistent with a death due to natural causes and could be the result of the embalming process. With regard to the poisoning charge, he felt that "without a post-mortem examination and toxicological studies, it is impossible to say absolutely that no poison was administered". At the same time, "there was no evidence that Mr Shastri had ingested any poison" and all available information showed that Shastri died from natural causes.

The accounts by CS Jha, LP Singh and CP Srivastava especially would have removed the last vestiges of doubts had it not been for a disclosure in 1998—which, to me, was the turning point in the Shastriji death mystery. In one swoop the veracity of the official account and those of former officials came under a dark cloud. There was neither a press report in India about it in those days nor a whisper in Parliament, but unknown to the people of India, something unfolded in Moscow.

That year, the Russian tabloid *Komsomolskaya Pravda* ran a story about Ahmed Sattarov, a butler to Soviet leaders from 1959 to 1972. It turned out that Sattarov was one of the Russian chefs who had, along with Mohammed Jan, prepared food for Shastri at the dacha. While Indian journalists gave it a miss,[1] the *Komsomolskaya Pravda* story was spotted by the Moscow correspondent of the British daily *The Telegraph*. On 18 February 1998, Alan Philps filed his story in the paper.

1 There is nothing on record to show that our Embassy in Moscow noted it either.

"When Lal Bahadur Shastri, the Indian Prime Minister, died suddenly in Tashkent (then part of the Soviet Union) in 1966, Mr Sattarov was arrested at 4 am on suspicion of poisoning him and thrown into jail," Philps revealed towards the end of his story—unaware of the implication of this hair-raising revelation. The official stand thus far had been that the suspicions of foul play emerged after Shastri's body was seen by his family members in India. But Sattarov's account turned this theory on its head. It was the Soviets who themselves started thinking along these lines as Shastri's corpse lay in the dacha.

SEVEN
A personal quest

IT WAS IN 2009 that I began picking up the threads in the Lal Bahadur Shastri death case. There was no public discourse about it in those days as the case had been dormant for decades. It just remained somewhere on the back of our collective minds, discussed in passing in private conversations every time Shastriji was remembered. What propelled me to do something was the constant nagging I was feeling ever since I had come to know about the revelation by the Russian butler in *The Daily Telegraph* of London. And there were repeated reminders in the course of my research about the disappearance of Netaji Subhas Chandra Bose. I grew up in south Delhi's residential hub for government officials, where the "mysteries" surrounding the deaths of these two national icons were usually discussed in the same breath.

In particular, I remember my maternal uncle referring to both. He was my personal connect, as it were, with the Shastri matter because he was one of the lakhs of regular people who thronged the PM's residence when his body was lying in state.

Therefore, it was but natural for me to dig around for the Shastriji case as I had done for the Netaji matter. By this time, India had been ushered in the Right to Information age like other democratic countries of the world. Ordinary citizens now had the unfettered right to seek information from their government. Of course, to respond or not was the Government's prerogative within the ambit of the Act. Most people used the RTI Act to access information concerning their private matters, but a few like me utilised it to procure information relating to matters of public importance.

I filed the first ever RTI application regarding Shastriji's death on 2 June 2009 with the Prime Minister's Office. Not expecting a bombshell, I did nonetheless hope to get much clarity and some documents as there was not much political sensitivity left in the case with the passage of time. I wrote in my application that while I expected the PMO to have all the information, in case they didn't, they could forward part/s of my RTI application to the concerned ministry/department/agency. I sought the following information/records:

- Please provide photocopies of all still classified files/papers relating to the death of the former Prime Minister. If the PMO is not holding any classified records on Shastriji's death, you may kindly state that fact.
- Did the PMO at any time destroy or lose records having a bearing on Shastriji's death and the subsequent developments relating to the incident? If yes, please provide details of the records destroyed/lost and the reasons thereof.
- Please detail the efforts made by the Government to ascertain the facts about Shastriji's death, including the allegations of foul play, and the outcome of those inquires.
- Please detail the information sent by the Government of erstwhile USSR on the death of the Prime Minister. The Soviets must have offered some details on the circumstances leading to Shastriji's death. If no information was shared, kindly state specifically.
- Please detail the findings of the post-mortem done in the USSR on the former Prime Minister's body to ascertain the cause of death. If no post-mortem was carried out in the USSR, please state specifically.

- Please detail the findings of the post-mortem done in India on the former Prime Minister's body to ascertain the cause of death. If no post-mortem was carried out in India, please state the reasons thereof.
- Please specify which Soviet and Indian physicians certified Shastriji's death and at what time and date.
- Whether any Indian physician accompanied Shastriji and whether he attended to Shastriji at the time of his demise?

In response, Director, PMO, replied that questions 4 and 5 were being transferred to the Foreign Secretary for an answer, and 3 and 5 to 8 to the Home Secretary. Nearly a month later, the PMO answered questions 1 and 2. The PMO, the response incredibly read, held "only one classified document" concerning the death of Shastri and even this could not be furnished under section 8 (1) (a) of RTI Act. Under this section, the Government was not obliged to part with information whose disclosure could "prejudicially affect the sovereignty and integrity of India, the security, strategic, scientific or economic interests of the State, relation with foreign State or lead to incitement of an offence".

Not very pleased, I conveyed this outcome to *The Times of India*. And so, on 11 July 2009, appeared a story in the daily headlined—"45 yrs on, Shastri's death a mystery". Even at the peak of the controversy decades earlier, the mainstream English newspapers had more or less kept away from this controversial matter, but here was this prominently placed story in India's most influential daily. The Shastri death mystery thus received a reboot in our times due to my RTI application.

The Ministry of External Affairs in the meanwhile responded that the "case was referred to both concerned Division in this Ministry as well as concerned Indian Mission in Moscow". The concerned Division in New Delhi astonishingly claimed that "they don't have any information on the subject matter", whereas the Indian embassy supplied the information that "main record available in the Mission is the report of the Joint Medical Investigation conducted by a team comprising Dr RN Chugh, Doctor-in-attendance to PM, and some senior Russian doctors". The Embassy stated that "as per records available" with them, there is "no other document from the erstwhile Soviet government detailing the circumstances leading to the demise of the former PM". I found this unbelievable. The Embassy also stated, in response to question number 5, that "as per the records available in the Mission, no post-mortem was conducted by the authorities on the body of the former Prime Minister".

The Ministry of Home Affairs sent me a series of responses, the first of which came from the PM Division in the ministry. They stated that some of my queries could be addressed by the statement the Government had made in December 1970. Another response stated that my queries were being forwarded to the National Archives and Delhi Police. The Office of the Additional Deputy Commissioner of Police, New Delhi District stated that they had "no such record related to the death of the former Prime Minister", which I think ruled out that any post-mortem was done in India. The Legal Cell in the Internal Security Division informed me that "as the subject matter relates to the death of the Prime Minister, VIP Security Section…may have information on the subject".

The Legal Cell forwarded my application to the VIP Security Section. I don't remember receiving any response from this section. I can't find any in my personal papers, unless it has been misplaced. I also can't locate any response from the National Archives, which in any case, usually tells RTI petitioners to come to the archive and search for the records themselves. To the best of my knowledge, there are no declassified files relating to Shastri's death in the National Archives. In the list of 64,906 files[1] declassified

1 This figure is few years old.

and sent to the National Archives Ministry of External Affairs, there are papers relating to the delegation sent to Tashkent, implementation of Tashkent Agreement, foreign comments about it and condolence messages on Shastri's death from Nepal, South Korea, Mongolia and other south east Asian countries.

As the law postulates, I thereafter filed an appeal with the Appellate authority in the PMO. Thanking the office for their response, I sought a review of their decision to deny me access to the sole classified record being held in the PMO regarding the Shastri death case. I made several submissions, including the need for transparency. However, the Appellate Authority in the PMO, a Joint Secretary, wrote back that much as she appreciated the point made by me in favour of transparency, "on perusal of the document in question and after giving the matter careful consideration", she was "satisfied that exemption sought under Section 8 (1) (a) has been invoked rightly". Following this denial, I took the matter to the Central Information Commission. This was in late 2009. I submitted to the CIC that I failed to understand how Section 8 (1) (a) of RTI Act applied to a document related to Shastri's death.

> It has been 44 long years since the Prime Minister died, and, therefore, there can be nothing in the record which might affect the sovereignty and integrity of India, her strategic interests, relation with a foreign State or lead to incitement of an offence in 2009. Relation with a foreign State cannot be affected since the foreign state in question, the USSR, does not exist. Its successor should not have any objection to release of any information about the USSR days. The Russian Federation has on several occasions disowned and even exposed the events that occurred in the USSR days.

I then argued that "to continue to keep the report secret will harm India's national interest as it will only fuel the conspiracy theories about the Prime Minister's death. That will only show the Government of India, and unfortunately our Russian friends in poor light". I cited a previous CIC ruling concerning the Subhas Chandra Bose papers my friends and I had sought to say that "it is against the RTI spirit to merely cite the Section 8 (I) (a) while stating the decision to withhold a particular record". On a matter of such national importance, I added, "it would have helped if they had offered some reasoning". My final argument was that the sole PMO record must be disclosed because:

> The public interest in disclosure in this case clearly outweighs the harm to the protected interests because making public the record about the Prime Minister's death will only help dispel the fallacies and bring a closure to the case.

As I pursued with the Central Information Commission the unsatisfactory response given by the PMO, I filed a fresh RTI application with the Ministry of External Affairs because I was not convinced by their response that the concerned division had no record about the only instance probably in the modern era of a head of government dying abroad. My application dated 21 July 2009 opened with a pressing comment that I hardly needed to "underline the importance" of what I was wanting to know. I put six specific questions covering different aspects of the matter so that the MEA could not dodge the issue this time.

- Kindly provide copies of the entire correspondence between the MEA and our Embassy in Moscow over the death of Prime Minister Lal Bahadur Shastri in Tashkent. This lot should include the details of telephone calls and the telegrams intimating the sudden death of the Prime Minister, circumstances leading to the death, arrangements to bring his body to India, etc. Our then Ambassador in Moscow, the late TN Kaul, or his deputies must have sent a number of reports on the matter. If no such correspondence/reports exist, please state that specifically.

- Kindly provide copies of the entire correspondence between the MEA and the Soviet foreign affairs ministry on the subject of the death of Prime Minister Shastri. If no such correspondence exists, please state that specifically.
- Please provide copies of the entire correspondence between our Embassy in Moscow and the Soviet foreign affairs ministry on the subject of the death of Prime Minister Shastri. If no such correspondence exists, please state that specifically.
- Please provide photocopy of the duly signed report of the Joint Medical Investigation conducted by a team comprising Dr RN Chug, Doctor-in-Attendance to PM, and the Soviet doctors. This report is available with our Mission in Moscow.
- Please provide information whether or not any records related to Shastriji's death were ever lost or destroyed by the Ministry and the Embassy. If yes, the details thereof.
- Please provide information whether or not the Ministry or the Embassy at any point of time made any attempts

> to investigate the allegations of foul play in Prime Minister's death. If yes, copies of the relevant records thereof.

The Ministry now gave me a flat answer that information sought by me "could not be disclosed under Section 8(1) (a) of RTI Act". All that they would tell me was that "no records with the Embassy of India, Moscow, relating to the demise of Prime Minister Shri Lal Bahadur Shastri in Tashkent on 11.01.66, or subsequent events, have either been destroyed or lost". The refusal of the ministry to provide me a copy of the duly signed report of the doctors deprived me of the chance to verify the allegation that Dr Gordon's name did not appear in the original report in Russian, as was alleged in Parliament in 1970.

After I wrote to the Appellate Authority and CIC intervened in the matter, the MEA in August 2011 wrote to me that "strenuous efforts" had yielded some additional information which they were furnishing. It was a poor photocopy of the official statement made in 1996 with English version of doctors' report attached to this statement. Strangely, in my papers I find a January 2009 response from the Rajya Sabha Secretariat stating that "as per existing records" no information was available regarding the doctors' report, which was tabled in Parliament and discussed by the lawmakers.

The Central Information Commission called a hearing with regard to the secret PMO document on 6 June 2011. I entered the chambers of Chief Information Commissioner Satyananda Mishra to find government officials looking grave as if Shastriji had died a week earlier. They made their arguments for not releasing the record and I made mine. At the end of it, Mishra ruled that he would like to see the record himself to see whether it substantiated the PMO's stand that information contained in it was "sensitive enough for India's security and foreign relations concerns. It is only after that that it should be possible to decide if the information should be disclosed or not."

As directed by the Chief Information Commissioner, the PMO officials furnished the record in a sealed envelope in the next hearing on 22 June. Mishra carefully went through the record as I watched. A Press Trust of India correspondent took notes of what the Chief Information Commissioner said thereafter. This was going to be flashed in the media. Mishra said that the document had "nothing to do directly" with Shastri's death. He ruled in favour of the PMO, giving this reason:

> The document comprises intelligence reports collected

> from different sources saying that a foreign country was spreading canards about former Prime Minister's death. The country mentioned here was not on good terms at that time but now we certainly have good relations. The document, if disclosed, has potential to adversely affect these relations.

This did not leave much to the imagination. The PMO record which was allowed to remain secret blamed the United States, rather the Central Intelligence Agency (CIA), for spreading the "lie" that Shastri's death was not natural. This whole matter about the Americans having a hand in whatever happened in Tashkent I am dealing with in the next chapter.

Thus, I failed in my attempt to get the desired information using the RTI act, though the effort did not go in vain. The government's refusal to release the records revived old suspicions. This resulted in the spotlight falling for the first time on the Shastri case in the mainstream electronic and print media. Shastri's family members and those having interest in the matter spoke out. While some of the charges were old, startling new information and perspectives also emerged. Senior Congress leader and Shastri's elder son, Anil Shastri, demanded the declassification of the file, and said: 'There is some suspicion in the minds of the people. Declassification would clear that doubt. Being a worker of the party which is in power, I would take up the issue at different levels of the Government.'[2] Kuldip Nayar stated: 'I still believe that Shastriji died of a heart attack. If the Government has any documents relating to his death, it should declassify it, otherwise it leads to suspicion of the Government.'[3]

Since the Government clammed up following this public outcry, suspicions kept on mounting. So much so that Nayar began to have doubts about the official version. On 2 October 2012 in a CNN-News 18 programme hosted by senior journalist Karan Thapar, Nayar disclosed that he first became apprehensive some time after the tragedy when a Member of Parliament raked up the charges of poisoning and TN Kaul, by then the Foreign Secretary, 'rang me up to issue a statement against it. He badgered me literally 4-5 times.' Nayar would repeat this when I accompanied Vivek Agnhotri to meet him during the filming of *The Tashkent Files*. His memory sharp as ever even though he is now 95, one of India's best known journalists has come to hold that something was wrong.

---

2 **Kuldip Nayar demands declassification of documents related to Shastri's death**, 18 July 2009. Accessed from: https://www.oneindia.com/2009/07/18/kuldipnayar-demands-declassification-of-documentsrelated.html.

3 Ibid.

The most significant development pertained to Ahmed Sattarov, the Russian butler attached to Shastri in Tashkent.

On 2 October 2013, Russian journalist Anton Vereshchagin wrote about him on the news website *Russia Beyond*. This was originally published in *Rossiyskaya Gazeta*, a Russian newspaper published by the Government of Russia. Referring to my RTI efforts, Vereshchagin carried an interview with Sattarov. It was revealed that after Shastri died, not only Sattarov but Mohammed Jan was also arrested as the Soviets suspected poisoning.

Sattarov remembered that early in the morning, soon after Shastri died, he was "woken by an officer of the Ninth Directorate of the KGB (responsible for VIP security)", who told him that "they suspected the Indian prime minister had been poisoned". Sattarov and three others were handcuffed and taken to a small town some 30 kilometres away from Tashkent. They were locked up in a basement. In Sattarov's words, as quoted in *Russia Beyond*:

> After a while, they brought the Indian chef who had cooked the Indian dishes for the banquet. We thought that it must have been that man who poisoned Shastri.

> We were so nervous that the hair on the temple of one of my colleagues turned gray before our eyes, and ever since I stutter.

Though Sattarov said that after six hours of confinement Kosygin himself entered the basement and personally apologised to them, saying that a "medical examination had shown that Shastri died a natural death from his fourth heart attack", it really did not add up. As per the statement made by the Government of India, no poisoning was ever suspected by Dr Chug and senior Russian doctors. They even signed Shastri's death report before the KGB picked up Sattarov, Mohammed Jan and others. If the doctors were really sure that Shastri's death was natural, as given out officially, what was the point in picking up the cooks on suspicions of poisoning? It was tell-tale indication that the KGB ignored the doctors' point of view, or what the doctors gave out officially was not entirely true. The very fact that Mohammed Jan's outspoken employer TN Kaul never uttered a word about his arrest, and that the Government never ever even alluded to it despite getting several chances meant that they were not being truthful. Sattarov's statement thus became the smoking gun in the Shastri death issue.

Incidentally, Sattarov ruled out the chances of

poisoning through food saying it 'could not get onto the banquet table or into the refrigerators of the apartments of the heads of state without undergoing a complete laboratory analysis' as the KGB 'controlled the whole banquet, including the quality of the food.' He asked whether there was really an opportunity for such an attempt? 'Every movement of the staff was under the supervision of the KGB and other intelligence agencies.' Sattarov was right. In 1991, an account of the Tashkent events by a former KGB officer was published in the *Soviet Land* magazine published by the Russian embassy in India. The officer revealed that the KGB was spying on both the Indian and Pakistani delegations in order to find out how much each country was willing to yield during the negotiations. The crucial thing reported by the *Soviet Land* piece was that:

> When Shastri started getting a seizure, the KGB was listening but decided not to alert his aides because that would give away their game and lead to a diplomatic showdown with India.[4]

4 **1965 War: Why India quit when it was winning**, Rakesh Krishnan Simha, Sep 02, 2015, *Russia Beyond.*

Sattarov's take that nothing could have been wrong with the food served to Shastri would have been acceptable to late Lalita Shastri. After speaking with Ram Nath, her suspicions were focused on the flask kept in his room from which her husband was given water. A few minutes after drinking the water he, according to her version in *Dharmyug* in 1970, felt 'heaviness in the head'. She emphasized, 'The flask did not come back to us from Tashkent.'

Lalita Shastri also told *Dharmyug* that her husband 'might have written something' for her in his missing diary. She was actually dropping a hint about something the family members couldn't muster the courage to reveal at that time because it was so explosive. According to CP Srivastava's book, on the morning of 10 January, Jagannath Sahai picked up a small piece of paper on which Shastri had written a couplet by poet Saqib Lakhnavi: *Bade shauq se sun raha tha zamana; Ham hi so gaye dastaan kehte kehte.* (The world was intently listening to me; only I fell asleep while narrating the story.) 'Had Shastriji a premonition of his death?' Srivastava posed. Shastri's family thinks somewhat differently. According to them, this was not the only scribble Shastri wrote on his last day. His eldest grandson, Sanjay Nath Singh, and others recall that after Shastri's personal belongings were returned to his family,

Lalita Shastri found a terse note hidden in his spectacle case. Written by Shastri in Hindi, it read: "I have been betrayed".

Where is that note now? The family members say that Lalita Shastri retained it for a while and then one day swallowed it in a frame of mind that was anything but normal. Why would she do that? The family members talk about a meeting Lalita had with a top personality who I'd rather have them name at some opportune moment. They say her attitude changed after this meeting—a showdown of some sort. From this time on, the safety of her living family members became the top priority for her. Lalita Shastri died in 1993 believing that her husband was killed. Her children and grandchildren believe till this day, and so do many others, that someone did not want the "truth" about Shastri's "death" to emerge.

They see a pattern in the fate that befell Dr RN Chugh and Ram Nath, the two most important witnesses to Shastri's death. A few days before the general elections in March 1977, in which Congress was expecting a rout amidst a rumour that the new Janata Party government might order a probe in the Shastri matter, a truck rammed into a car killing Dr RN Chugh, his wife and their eldest son. The daughter survived but was crippled for life. Around the same time, the family says, Ram Nath met

Lalita Shastri and told her that he was going to "unburden" himself. Thereafter, he left the Shastris' residence and was hit by a bus. He survived but his legs were amputated. He would never talk about the Shastri case ever again. About Ram Nath, I heard from Shastriji's family. But the matter of Dr Chugh's horrific accident was even raised in Parliament more than once. CPM parliamentarian Jyotirmoy Basu,[5] who was jailed at the instance of Indira Gandhi in 1975, described the accident in the Lok Sabha on 24 June 1977 when atrocities committed during the Emergency were being discussed. The truck hit the car from behind. After the impact, Dr Chugh came out of the car to assess the damage, only to be hit by the same truck again in what did not appear to be a regular accident.

---

5 Jyotirmoy Bose 'was not a prominent leader in the party echelon. Moreover, there is a widespread belief, Indira got the approval of some senior leaders of the CPI-M to arrest him as some of his startling accusations against her put the Prime Minister on the wrong foot'. [Samit Kar, **The Black Day**, *Mainstream*, VOL LIV No 30, 16 July 2016].

EIGHT

A world of conspiracies

OUR MINDS HAVE been conditioned in such a way that any mention of conspiracy theories instinctively takes our thoughts to the outlandish claims made over the controversies surrounding the fate of Subhas Chandra Bose and Lal Bahadur Shastri. While there is no denying that the Netaji death mystery, and to an extent Shastri death case too, entail a wide range of crazy conspiracy theories, these two do not monopolise this phenomenon. Some six years before the term "conspiracy theory" was included in the Oxford English Dictionary, a most atrocious one was propounded over the assassination of former Prime Minister Rajiv Gandhi. We don't find any reference to it when conspiracy theories are discussed, because it is far easier to mock those related to Netaji or Shastriji.

Soon after the news of the heart-wrenching tragedy

came in from Sriperumbudur, hundreds of understandably angry Congress party workers gathered on the streets of Delhi. Steve Coll, then South Asia bureau chief for *The Washington Post*, reported on 22 May 1991 that these workers "chanted slogans against the CIA, accusing the US intelligence agency of engineering the assassination". Coll, a Pulitzer Prize winner with keen interest in the CIA,[1] added that it was "often blamed by India's conspiracy-minded political activists for a wide variety of the country's ills".[2]

On June 14, Coll filed another story which reported that even India's elite were blaming the CIA. The belief was "pervasive even among Indian politicians, bureaucrats, academics and journalists who have lived or traveled in the West".[3] This belief, Coll added, appeared to have arisen "not from evidence or even coherent speculation, but from a deep-seated emotional conviction". Coll cited the example of a 2,000 word assessment titled "Day of the Jackal" in the weekly *Sunday Observer* by Sudheendra

1 Coll first won the Pulitzer in 1990 and then in 2005 for his book **Ghost Wars: The Secret History of the CIA**. He is currently the dean of the Columbia University Graduate School of Journalism.

2 Steve Coll, **Bomb kills India's ex-premier Gandhi**, *The Washington Post*, 22 May 1991.

3 Steve Coll, **India elite see CIA plot in Rajiv killing**, *Houston Chronicle*, 16 June 1991 (The story originally appeared in *The Washington Post* 2 days earlier).

Kulkarni—counted among the most well-known thinkers in India today. Kulkarni postulated that it was the desire of the US "to ensure that India, Pakistan, and Bangladesh remain impoverished, weak, and unstable".

The *Post* piece led to a discussion in the US House of Representatives on 26 June 1991. Doug Bereuter—a Republican from Nebraska who would in 2004 break ranks with his party to oppose the war against Iraq—spoke about "a bizarre Indian rationale for this fantastic theory". He referred to the views of well-educated Indians that "the CIA killed Gandhi because he was a strong leader who would have transformed India into a great world power that would have challenged the United States on the international stage". Bereuter then tore into this charge:

> One hardly knows where to begin in addressing such a patently ridiculous and irresponsible assertion; however, even such ridiculous charges might be believed or be given some credibility in the absence of a denial. Therefore, the subject needs to be addressed and I will do so as a Member of the House Select Committee on Intelligence. Resisting the obvious temptation to recommend a massive course of group psychotherapy for some of the Indian ruling elite, let me inject one or two important facts or elements for sanity into this febrile, paranoid delusion. First of all,

> assassination is specifically prohibited by a Presidential directive.... the rationale cited to explain why we should want to see Mr Gandhi dead is totally inconsistent with the facts and with rational thought. Far from wanting to destabilize India and see it perpetually locked in poverty, United States policies and programs are directed toward helping India achieve just the opposite. Both the executive branch and Congress have long supported a policy of trying to promote stability in the Indian subcontinent.[4]

Doug Bereuter explained that not only was there a ban on political assassinations in the US, even covert actions, the category of intelligence activities in which any questions about assassination conceivably could arise, were carefully reviewed within the CIA and at the sub-Cabinet and Cabinet level in the National Security Council (NSC) review process. "The President himself is usually present during the Cabinet-level NSC review. Ultimately, the President must approve every covert action because he must sign a written document certifying that each covert action is important to the national security of the United States". He added that the House and Senate Intelligence

4 Congressional Record, 102nd Congress (1991-1992), House of Representatives, 26 June 1991, page H5201.

Committees scrupulously reviewed each covert action authorised by the President.

At the time of Rajiv Gandhi's assassination, George H W Bush, a former CIA director, was the President. While the relations between India and America in those days were nothing like they became during the presidency of Bush's son and namesake, the senior Bush was nonetheless favourbly disposed towards Rajiv Gandhi at a personal level. According to *The New York Times*, Bush called the assassination 'appalling' and said 'he mourned the loss of a friend and world leader.' Bush said his wife and he were close to Sonia and Rajiv. 'That this is a real tragedy.' Even though Bush's predecessor, Ronald Reagan (1981-1989), was engaged in a fight to finish with the USSR, and India was pro-Soviet Union, the red carpet was rolled out at the White House to welcome both Indira Gandhi and Rajiv Gandhi. Courtesies and respect due to the leaders of a nation of the size and importance of India were extended to them. Visuals from that time show Reagan seeing Rajiv Gandhi off, sheltering him from the pouring rain with an umbrella held by elderly Reagan himself. At Rajiv's request, Reagan also granted a presidential pardon to his childhood friend Adil Shahryar, who was serving a 35-year sentence for offences which included an attempt to blow up a ship. Incidentally, an executive order signed in 1981 by Reagan barred any "person employed by or acting on behalf of the United States Government" from conspiring or carrying out "political assassination".

As Bereuter underlined in the House of Representatives: "As a member of the House Intelligence Committee, I can assure the House that we are particularly careful to assure ourselves that these covert programs and activities do not involve assassination by direct or by any indirect means. That is why I was especially struck by the preposterous assertion in this news report that the CIA was somehow behind the tragic death of Rajiv Gandhi". He emphasised that he brought up this matter because he wanted "the people of India to know the facts behind this cynical fable and to have those assurances from a member of the House Select Committee on Intelligence".[5]

> I hope the Indian people learn these facts and this assurance, for they are the whole truth and nothing but the truth. The United States of America had no direct or indirect role in the assassination of Rajiv Gandhi. Our Government and the American people deplore this terrible act and share the grief of the people of India over this tragic and senseless act.[6]

---

5 Ibid.
6 Ibid.

Despite this reasonable explanation and such a background of good personal relations between Indian and American heads of government, the conspiracy theorists in India kept on singing the old tune. All limits were crossed when the Indian government itself backed the conspiracy theory, unmindful of the havoc it could wreak on the Indo-US relations. This was absolutely shocking because at the same time the Americans were being accused of having a hand in the assassination, Prime Minister Narasimha Rao wrote a letter to President Bush about the security of Rahul Gandhi, then studying at Harvard. "I have ventured to do so," Rao wrote, "knowing the warmth of your friendship as also the affection that Mrs Bush and you had for Mr Rajiv Gandhi and his family". Rao's letter was quoted by Vinay Sitapati, writer of *Half Lion: How PV Narasimha Rao Transformed India* in an interview with *The Telegraph* of Kolkata in 2016. Stating that Indian security agencies believed that Sikh extremists were plotting to kill Rahul, Rao sought enhanced security for Rahul by way of assigning him a trained person "who has also the necessary intelligence backing of various agencies, and effective means of communication".[7]

---

7 Rasheed Kidwai, **The years when Narasimha Rao played lion and mouse with Sonia**, *The Telegraph*, 28 June 2016.

In stark contrast, when the Rajya Sabha was discussing the Rajiv Gandhi assassination case on 26 July 1991, Home Minister SB Chavan stood up to say that while the LTTE connection was a clear possibility, the hand of a superpower could not be ruled out. Basing the Government's hypothesis on an exaggerated notion about Rajiv Gandhi's standing in the comity of nations, Chavan went on to assert that 'the leadership of the Third World happens to be, whether we like it or not, with India and when we meant India, it was Rajiv Gandhi and none else.'

This, the Home Minister of India, proclaimed, was an 'irritant to some of the countries who are now left almost unchallenged as a super power.'

> Now, a point which we have to consider is, if he was going to emerge as the leader of the third world, whether he should be allowed to remain or he was to be finished so that India would not have any leader of his stature who could possibly take up the issue and fight with the super powers. So this is the kind of suspicion that I have, and it becomes all the more necessary that we have to go deep into the matter and try to find out who are the conspirators against whom we can say that, these are

> the conspirators who are at the root of the assassination of Rajiv Gandhi.[8]

This thinking on the part of the Government coupled with the report of Justice MC Jain Commission of inquiry led to the formation of a Multi-Disciplinary Monitoring Agency (MDMA), in 1998, with top officers drawn from the Research and Analysis Wing, Intelligence Bureau, Directorate of Military Intelligence, Central Bureau of Investigation, Directorate of Enforcement, etc. From that time till today, this high-powered group has been chasing the mirage of "international conspiracy" on taxpayers' money. Since this "conspiracy" exists only in the minds of some people, no evidence of any sort has till date been found. And having known a former CBI Director who was associated with the investigation into the assassination, I can assure you nothing ever will. The MDMA's work goes on and on, years after the LTTE owned up its crime and the chief plotters and executers died or were killed. And all along we have been hearing eminent historians and others saying that to inquire into Subhas Bose's death

8 Raya Sabha proceeding record, Session Number 159, 26 July 1991, pages 203-4, Clarifications on the statement regarding escape from the custody and subsequent death of Shanmugam, one of the accused in the Rajiv Gandhi assassination case.

was futile, a waste of time and public money. I anticipate that this logic will resurface when the Shastriji matter gets registered on the national conscious with the release of *The Tashkent Files*.

This lengthy backgrounder was necessary before assessing the first among the various conspiracy theories about Shastri's death—that the United States had something to do with it.

The first time it happened, though not directly, was in October 1974, when a New Delhi political commentator claimed in an article in *The Times of India* that the CIA stole in 1965 a comprehensive clinical report on Lal Bahadur Shastri's blood analysis for its dossier on the then Prime Minister. Government of India denied having any knowledge about it and never again was this matter heard. The government denial came at a time when the CIA was getting a lot of dirty press in India, as Steve Coll rightly commented. The momentum started building up in the 1960s and peaked in the 1970s. In part, it was the result of a conscious decision to distract the attention of the Indian people from holding their leadership accountable for their failures, inability to rescue India from grinding poverty, in particular.

And so we had a sort of "golden era" for Indian conspiracy theorists in those days. The Congress leaders were better than the best and from top to bottom every leader floated one theory or another targeting the CIA. In 1972 Congress President Shankar Dayal Sharma—later the President of India—told the media that the US spy agency was disrupting the socio-economic life of our country. On 20 October, in Bhopal the same year, he accused the agency of colluding with opposition parties to 'create chaos and frustrate our efforts to banish poverty'. On 29 November 1974, twenty-one Congress members of Parliament accused the US and the CIA of subverting India's internal situation. Though they did not name the Jayaprakash Narayan-led movement in Bihar and other parts of the country, they implied that the movement was getting help from the USA and its agency to upset the process of democracy in the country. In fact, I remember seeing declassified records in the National Archives in Delhi where NRIs and PIOs in America who were supporting the JP moment were characterised as CIA agents. It was in that turbulent era that Piloo Mody performed a most comical antic which is remembered till date. He turned up in Parliament wearing a placard that read: "I am a CIA agent".[9]

---

9 On 13 November 1972, Communist Party of India leader Bhupesh Gupta said that if Mody was being serious, "he should be taken into custody" as his act was "derogatory to Parliament" and "the CIA is against our country".

In those days, the Congress leaders, with the backing of Prime Minister Indira Gandhi, whipped up passions in the country to such an extent that an American hand was seen behind small demonstrations in remote corners of the country. At the same time, Janus-faced Congress leaders and senior government officials, military, civil and intelligence, did not have any qualms about quietly sending their children and relatives to America for the bright prospects the world's most prosperous nation offered.

To a lesser degree, the tradition continues in our times. The undisputed king of the conspiracists in India today is Osama Bin Laden sympathiser Digvijaya Singh. Popularly called "Diggy Raja", this senior Congress leader and a former Chief Minister has helped spread theories as outrageous and anti-national as the one alleging that 26/11 was carried out by the Indian Intelligence Bureau in cahoots with the CIA and Mossad, the Israeli intelligence agency. On the scale of one to ten of most absurd conspiracy theories ever, this one probably ranks with the ones that claim that the George Bush administration itself plotted 9/11 or that it was result of a Jewish conspiracy. Come to think of it, after the CIA, the Mossad has been turned into a sort of bugbear by many conspiracists from the Indian subcontinent. In the course of proceedings of Jain Commission of Inquiry, it was revealed that in June 1991, then Indian Foreign Secretary met the Palestinian ambassador in India. The ambassador claimed that "they had seen the movement of Mossad agents in India, including towards Madras". He said that if one was looking for a link, "it was the CIA/Mossad/LTTE link"[10] to Rajiv Gandhi's assassination earlier that year. The Indian side apparently believed this. Justice Jain wrote in his report that this meeting "amply borne out that there was an international plot to assassinate Rajiv Gandhi and that it was a Mossad/LTTE/CIA link".[11] He also gave much credence to a telegram sent by the Indian Ambassador in Tunis to New Delhi in September 1991 that he got a tipoff from PLO president Yasser Arafat that he had information Rajiv faced danger to his life from forces inside and outside India. Justice Jain wrote that "the CIA seems to have a track-record of covert operations for destabilising governments while indulging in assassination plots or otherwise as reported in the print media.... It is in this background of the CIA's alleged track-record that Arafat's utterances have to be evaluated".[12]

---

10 Charu Lata Joshi, **Finally All Fingers Point To A Foreign Hand**, *Outlook*, 20 July 1998.

11 Ibid.

12 Ibid.

A clear pattern emerges when one notes that at different points in time everything is blamed on the Americans—from Rajiv's assassination to 26/11; from JP's movement to Anna Hazare's fast. When in 2011, the Congress party "hinted at an American hand behind Anna Hazare-led protests",[13] most observers just laughed it away—not realising that it was symptomatic of a deep-seated malaise. In the annals of the Bose mystery there was a case of a former MEA official, Dr Satyanarain Sinha. He told an inquiry panel probing Subhas Bose's death that when he tried to sensitise Prime Minister Nehru about Bose's presence in the USSR after he was reported dead, the PM told him that "this is American propaganda". Sinha further claimed that the PM called him an "American agent". My eighteen years of research into the Bose disappearance tells me that it is anything but an American propaganda.

In 2009, everyone came to know about the existence of a secret document in the possession of the PMO, which was denied to me under the RTI Act, and which reportedly states that the US spy agency spread false rumours about Shastri's death. With this disclosure, the CIA-hand theory

---

13 **Congress hints at US hand in Anna Hazare protest**, *The Times of India*, 18 August 2011.

was revived. A little later, it came to be viewed in the context of a sensational claim which first appeared in 2000 in an obscure book published in America. Written by Gregory Douglas, *Conversations with the Crow* (Basilisk Press) contained transcripts of his conversations with Robert Trumbull Crowley, who had retired from the CIA after serving for decades in its Directorate of Plans, better known as the "Department of Dirty Tricks". According to Douglas, Crowley first contacted him in 1993 when he found out about his plan to publish his first book which was about Heinrich Müller, the former head of the Gestapo. Over a period of time, Crowley, who passed away in 2000, divulged a number of state secrets to Douglás, going by his claim. In an expletive-laden rant, Crowley claimed that the CIA was responsible for Shastri's killing as well as downing of Air-India's Boeing 707 carrying nuclear scientist Homi Bhabha, thirteen days after the tragedy in Tashkent.

> We had trouble, you know, with India back in the 60s when they got uppity and started work on an atomic bomb. Loud mouthed cow-lovers bragging about how clever they were and how they, too, were going to be a great power in the world. The thing is, they were getting into bed with the Russians. Of course, Pakistan was in

> bed with the chinks, so India had to find another bed partner. And we did not want them to have any kind of nuclear weaponry because God knows what they would have done with it. ...Oh, yes, and their head expert was fully capable of building a bomb and we knew just what he was up to. He was warned several times but what an arrogant prick that one was. ...name was Homi Bhabha. That one was dangerous, believe me. He had an unfortunate accident. He was flying to Vienna to stir up more trouble, when his 707 had a bomb go off in the cargo hold and they all came down on a high mountain way up in the Alps. No real evidence and the world was much safer.[14]

With regard to Shastri, Crowley rattled off the following to Douglas:

> And we nailed Shastri as well. Another cow-loving raghead. Gregory, you say you don't know about these people. Believe me, they were close to getting a bomb and so what if they nuked their deadly Paki enemies? So what?...Shastri was a political type who started the

14 *TBR News*, 14 August 2010, accessed from: http://www.tbrnews.org/tbr-news-august-14-2010/.

> program in the first place. Babha was a genius and he could get things done, so we aced both of them.[15]

How credible is this piece of loose talk, taking it at face value? For a start, Crowley was inflicted with the Alzheimer's disease, which destroys memory and other important mental functions over a period of time. So we are not sure in what state of mind he was when he made those wild charges in language a professional of his level is most unlikely to use, especially at an age when even the most hot-headed ones mellow down. At that, Gregory Douglas is known for making a claim that Heinrich Müller, chief of Hitler's Gestapo and a major Nazi war criminal, was recruited by the CIA after the war. The CIA has declassified its file on Müller and it says no such thing. It details the efforts to find him after his disappearance in 1945. The CIA did not know Müller's whereabouts at any point after the war, the file makes it clear. But in an interview with tabloid *The Spotlight* on 6 January 1997, Douglas claimed that he met Müller in 1965. 'He was a US citizen and lived here until his death.' Again, it is unthinkable that the US, which has a sizeable and most influential Jewish population, would shelter

---

15 Ibid.

someone who was involved in the planning and execution of the Holocaust. It is true that the US secretly recruited German scientists after the war, but none of them were in the league of the notorious Müller. On top of this, what with a robust declassification regime on one hand, and media's and former officials' proclivity to publicise state secrets on the other, it is very difficult to keep a lid on such a horrendous secret in America if it really was the case.

It is to be noted that America leads the world in the field of declassification. The CIA is the only foreign intelligence agency in the world which regularly releases its records. It is also covered by the FOIA (Freedom of Information Act). Even foreigners can seek information from the agency under this act. I personally applied for and received information and documents concerning Subhas Chandra Bose from the CIA. Under the RTI Act of India, our own intelligence agencies are exempt from giving any information, unless in very rare cases when there are claims of human rights abuse. (One cannot file an RTI application with either R&AW or IB concerning the Shastri case therefore.) The US State Department is bound by law since 1861 to publish official documented historical records of major foreign policy decisions and significant diplomatic activity of the United States Government 30 years after their occurrence. The Foreign Relations of the

United States (FRUS) Series offer the most authentic records concerning major US foreign policy decisions and significant diplomatic activity. In addition, there are Presidential libraries which are repositories for preserving and making available to public the records and other historical materials relating to every US President.

There are several declassified CIA, State Department and even Presidential records[16] where Shastriji is discussed prominently or in passing. I personally accessed some of the CIA records at the US National Archives in Maryland, where millions of records declassified by the agency can be viewed by anyone. In my limited capacity, I undertook a survey of all these records in the backdrop of the conspiracy theory that America might have something to do with his death because he wanted India to go nuclear.

Shastri's name first figures in the CIA reports from the time when Jawaharlal Nehru's health was failing. A special report dated 24 January 1964 titled "An ailing Nehru and Indian leadership" noted that "illness has removed Jawaharlal Nehru from the day-to-day control of the Indian Government". The report said that "the

---

16 CIA's records can be accessed from the agency's Electronic Reading Room: https://www.cia.gov/library/readingroom/home.
State Department records can be accessed from the Office of the Historian website: https://history.state.gov/.
The website of the LBJ Presidential Library hosts the records and sound recordings cited in this book. http://www.lbjlibrary.org/.

man most likely to be chosen as Nehru's successor is Lal Bahadur Shastri, a trusted political veteran who would carry on the main lines of Nehru's policies". In CIA's view, Shastri was "generally well liked within the party", had "a reputation as a conciliator", and "the parliamentary experience necessary to do the job". The agency saw a few disabilities in Shastri. Among them were "his colourlessness and his frailness" and "unproven capacity for decisions". The agency thought at this stage, that as prime minister "Shastri's politics would be cautious, pragmatic, and moderate" and in foreign affairs domain he was likely to stick to non-alignment.

A Central Intelligence Bulletin issued on 1 June 1964 reported that "the way has apparently been cleared for moderate 59-year-old Lal Bahadur Shastri to succeed to the prime ministership" days after Nehru passed away. On 2 June, it was observed that Shastri brought to the prime ministership many valuable assets. "He is skilled in the art of compromise and has a well-developed facility for deft political maneuver". The bulletin for 10 June briefly touched upon the new Cabinet, which was "substantially like the group presided over by Nehru during his last months in office". It commented that Shastri was likely to be more flexible than Nehru was on such matters as the Kashmir problem.

In July 1964, when Shastri was operating from his residence in the wake of a mild heart attack, the CIA observed that his government was "following India's tested policies of political, economic, and military balance between both East and West". On 25 February 1965, the Director of CIA wrote a memorandum on the "likelihood of Indian development of nuclear weapons". It stated that despite the October 1964 Chinese explosion, India had "publicly reaffirmed its intent not to produce nuclear weapons". It added that "the Congress Party, at Shastri's behest, formally adopted a statement of policy against the production of such weapons".

It would be pertinent here to refer to a confidential letter written by Homi Bhabha on 13 April 1964 to Shastri, then virtually running the government for Nehru. The letter drew Shastri's attention to a news item titled "India can make a Bomb" published in a British newspaper. Bhabha then made this self-explanatory comment underlining India's position:

> That we could make an atomic bomb, if we wanted to, has been stated openly for quite some time, and the President himself said so in a speech to Parliament some years ago. That we are striving to obtain the Government's decision to do so is however false. As you are aware, since

> you deal with atomic energy matters, no paper has been sent either to you or to the Prime Minister suggesting that we take up the manufacture of atomic weapons, and even the Atomic Energy Commission has had no paper to this effect before it. The article in *The Sunday Telegraph* appears to be full of misinformation, and I do not know whether we should contradict it or simply remain quiet.[17]

The issue was again discussed in a Special National Intelligence Estimate the CIA circulated among top US policy makers on 21 October 1965. Such estimates contained authoritative assessments of the intelligence related to a particular national security issue. It was felt that if India decided to develop nuclear weapons, it "could conduct its first test within few months". But as a prelude, there had to be advance work on weapon design, technology and a testing site. "We have no evidence that such activities are well advanced", the estimate read.

Stating that India's case for nuclear weapons had been strengthened by the war with Pakistan, the CIA concluded that Shastri did not wish to do so. "His immediate course

17 National Archives of India, Ministry of External Affairs, File No. XPP/3073/36/64.

of action will probably be to keep India's diplomatic and technical options open. During this period, he will weigh the assurances, inducements, and pressures that are forthcoming from the great powers. He will almost certainly avoid commitments to international agreements which might curtail India's options, and he will support technical efforts to shorten the time between an affirmative decision and the detonation of a first device". In its final estimate, the CIA concluded that the Shastri government was "probably predisposed to postpone a decision" for some time "in return for a continued high level of US economic aid, a renewal of military assistance, and a foregoing of pressure on the Kashmir issue".

This assessment that the Shastri government, at the end of 1965, was not actively working on developing nuclear weapons goes against Crowley's fantastic claim that fearing that India was on the verge of going nuclear, the CIA blew up an entire Boeing 707 in the French Alps just to get Bhabha. There is no evidence to back the claim that the 24 January 1966 crash of Air India Flight 101 Kanchenjunga was engineered. The crash was investigated by the Bureau of Enquiry and Analysis for Civil Aviation Safety (BEA), the French government agency responsible for investigating aviation accidents. Its 16-page report was released in 1968 after more than a year of inquiry. The transcript of the talk between the pilot-in-command and the radar controller shows that there were black clouds over the Mont Blanc, the highest mountain in Europe at 15,777 feet. As it made a descent toward Geneva International Airport, the plane struck the Mont Blanc at an elevation of 15,585 feet. The experts who visited the crash location more than once and studied the debris of the aircraft concluded that everything pointed to a crash caused by an impact with the ground. The most likely hypothesis as to what caused this as per the BEA report was that either the pilot miscalculated his position in relation to the Mont Blanc, or misunderstood the communication from the controller, thinking that he had passed the ridge leading to the summit. This information is gleaned from the BEA report, details given on online portal "Aviation Safety Network"[18] (which provides authoritative information on airline accidents) and observations made by top aviation journalist David Cenciotti on "The Aviationist",[19] one of the world's most popular aviation sites.

Rome-based Cenciotti wrote about the Bhabha death conspiracy theory in April 2009 when it was claimed that

18 https://aviation-safety.net/database/record.php?id=19660124-0.

19 https://theaviationist.com/2009/04/21/air-india-101-conspiracy-theory/.

the plane might have been hit by an Italian aircraft or missile. A story appearing in the *Daily News & Analysis* (Mumbai) attributed this theory to Daniel Roche, another aviation enthusiast who had spent years researching and collecting the remnants of the plane from Mont Blanc. "If Kanchenjunga had crashed in the mountain, there should have been huge fire and explosion as there was 41,000 tonnes of fuel in the aircraft, but that was not the case. Just two minutes before the crash, the aircraft was at 6,000 feet above the ground. According to me, it collided with an Italian aircraft and as there is very little oxygen at that height, there was no combustion that could cause an explosion", the paper quoted him saying. "There were news reports that time about an Italian aircraft that had gone missing the same day. There are chances that it collided into the aircraft. I managed to find a fuel tank of the Italian plane with inscriptions on it",[20] Roche added. Cenciotti responded, after due searches of records, that the reports of Italian aircraft gone missing the same day were "probably true" but were "not related to the Air India crash". Regarding the Kanchenjunga tragedy, he wrote

---

20 Naveeta Singh, **Was Homi Bhabha's plane hit by Italian aircraft?** *DNA*, 16 April 2009.

that he did not think it was shot down by the Italian air force (ItAF).

> First of all because evidence would be found; second because the investigation report did not mention any possibility the aircraft was destroyed by anything else than the impact with the mountain. Third, if the ItAF was interested in downing the aircraft, why not do that far from the boundaries with other two nations? It would have been far easier to shoot it down above the Sea, in southern Italy or above the Adriatic.[21]

Returning to the narrative regarding Shastri as emerging from the American records, on 28 May 1965, the CIA produced a 14-page, mostly laudatory, special report titled "Shastri's first year as India's Prime Minister". It read:

---

21 Cenciotti returned to the subject on *The Aviationist* in September 2011 after Roche sent him pictures of the aircraft parts he had found on the glacier he said proved his theory of a collision with an Italian fighter jet. "I've already written in my previous article what I think about the crash. Plane crash investigations require experts in various fields. They must be performed in accordance with specific procedures and protocols, that cover also how evidences must be collected and preserved. So, regardless what Daniel believes, I still think the official report of the French BEA says it all about the reasons of the crash of the Air India 101 flight," Cenciotti wrote.

A year after Nehru's fatal stroke, the style of the Indian Government and the ruling Congress Party has changed rather markedly. Most striking is the transformation of the office of the prime minister, which used to embody Nehru's imperious, cosmopolitan personality but now reflects the colourless, homespun, consensus-minded character of his successor as leader of 470 million Indians, Lal Bahadur Shastri. Despite moments when it seemed that Shastri might be overwhelmed by the demands and complexities of the office, his position now is at least as strong and possibly a bit stronger than when the party caucus assembled by Congress Party President Kamaraj chose him to be prime minister last June... Shastri, as the product of British India, British jails, Indian poverty, and the independence movement, embodies India's mood and the mood of its ruling party in the immediate post-Nehru period. He is doing a reasonably good job of giving the country the type of leadership it seems to want and the only type of leadership its ruling party would permit at this time, only one year after Nehru. The condition which led to his choice last June—the absence of an alternative candidate acceptable to the party as a whole—remains, and Shastri gives every indication of intending to be more than a mere caretaker prime minister.

The report further said that Shastri's foreign policies were "virtually indistinguishable from Nehru's, at least the post-1962, post-Chinese invasion Nehru". The reference here was to Nehru's secret approach to John F Kennedy, seeking military assistance for India's defence against the Chinese onslaught. The post-1962 war period was marked by close collaboration between the CIA and IB, which was yet to be bifurcated to form R&AW. In fact, a report published in *Hindustan Times* in March 1975 stated that in the sixties the CIA had "trained senior Indian intelligence officers and helped build the nucleus of India's counter-intelligence network".[22]

Unknown to people of India in those days, CIA's Top Secret U-2 spy plane programme received support from India, and from 1964 onwards CIA-IB ran joint covert missions against the Chinese. In the latter instance, CIA and IB personnel operated on Nanda Devi mountain in the Himalayas so that they could spy on Chinese missile activity in the Sinkiang region. They installed a nuclear-fuelled remote sensing device on the peak in 1965 but a subsequent blizzard caused the device to go missing at a

---

22 Chand Joshi, **CIA coached Indians on intelligence**, *Hindustan Times*, 14 March 1975.

height of about 23,000 ft. A new device was taken to the same area and duly installed on a neighbouring peak in 1967. The operations were carried out with the approval of Lal Bahadur Shastri and Indira Gandhi. So, it's not too surprising to see CIA's 28 May 1965 report stating that under Shastri's rule, India's "relations with the United States have been friendly, despite the occasional emotional outbursts of his foreign minister and Shastri's unhappiness with some aspects of US policy in Southeast Asia".

By late 1965, CIA's attention had turned to India-Pakistan tensions and the Soviet attempts to douse the fire. The Central Intelligence Bulletin for 20 September 1965 reported that Kosygin had invited both Ayub and Shastri to meet on Soviet soil to reach agreement on the restoration of peace. The Soviet proposal included a suggestion that Kosygin himself would participate in the talks if the two prime parties wished. In CIA's estimate, "this dramatic extension of Moscow's previous offers of its 'good offices' to help end hostilities reflects growing Soviet concern over the possible consequences of deeper Chinese involvement in the crisis".

The next day, the US Embassy in New Delhi sent a telegram to the Department of State in Washington, DC, informing them that Foreign Secretary LK Jha had called Ambassador Bowles just after the Soviet proposal for direct negotiations in Tashkent. Jha had called up at the instance of Prime Minister Shastri to explain India's position in regard to ceasefire resolution and "to inquire urgently how US would react to an Indian acceptance in principle of Soviet proposal for mediation".

> Jha requested at earliest possible moment reactions of US government since it was necessary to give Soviets answer on Wednesday well before Chinese deadline expires. What, he asked, would we think of such a meeting? Would we consider it helpful, or would it seem to bring Soviets into a role that would not be in US interests? Shastri would appreciate getting our views on highly confidential basis soonest. Jha added that Kosygin was pushing India hard for a favourable answer.

The Department authorised Bowles to respond to Jha's questions concerning the Soviet offer to mediate by expressing appreciation for being consulted, and by indicating that the US government still considered that the best hope for solution to the conflict lay in action through the United Nations.

The Central Intelligence Bulletin of 28 December 1965 reiterated the agency's earlier position that Soviet attempts to restore peace in the Indian subcontinent were inspired by a desire to prevent rival China from exploiting 'unrest on the subcontinent'.

That Shastri had positive vibes towards America is proven by his letter to President Lyndon Johnson on 6 January 1966 from Tashkent. Thanking Johnson for help to meet the critical shortage of foodgrains in India, Shastri praised his effort "to bring about a peace in Vietnam". About the talks with President Ayub, he wrote that while there were difficult issues, he hoped things would change and "there will be a different atmosphere in which it will be easier to resolve and reconcile our differences". At the end, Shastri stated that he and his wife were looking forward to their visit to the US.

After this stage we have documents and sound recordings made available by LBJ Presidential Library giving us a rare insight into the White House's reaction to Shastri's death. At 5:45 pm on Monday, 10 January 1966, the White House press officer read out the following statement of the US President: "Our nation mourns the death of Prime Minister Lal Bahadur Shastri of India. As the leader of the world's largest democracy, he had already gained a special place in American hearts. His tragic loss, after fruitful discussions at Tashkent, is a grievous blow to the hopes of mankind for peace and progress". The message went on to describe Shastri as "a fitting successor to Pandit Nehru", who held aloft "the highest ideals of Indian democracy". The statement ended with the tribute that Shastri's "modesty in high office did not conceal his strength and wisdom as the recognised leader of his people. The world is a smaller place without him, and our hearts go out to his family and to the people of India".

Going by the American President's Daily Diary entry for 10 January 1966 from about 6.25 pm to well past 11 in the night, Johnson several times consulted with Secretary of State Dean Rusk and others on who should represent US at Shastri's funeral; whether Johnson should himself go; whether it was definite protocol for the Vice President of the US to attend; what would be Indian reaction, etc. Since Johnson secretly recorded his conversations, many of these conversations concerning Shastri's death have been made public by the LBJ Presidential Library. The world's most powerful person can be heard speaking his mind in these uncensored tapes which were never meant to go public. Johnson and his officials are sombre and respectful as they discuss Shastri's funeral in these recordings. In one of them (citation number: 9475), Johnson asks: 'Had it been through the years, (can you find out)—had it been a custom of the United States to send the highest ranking official or the Vice President to these funerals?' Dean Rusk answers: 'Well, we've had relatively few cases of prime ministers dying in office.' Not just this, the library has also made public the transcript of the audio diary of Lady Bird Johnson. The President's wife was clearly pained by the passing away of Shastri because she was preparing to host him and Lalita Shastri in the White House.

> All afternoon I worked.... Sometime, I don't remember exactly when, the phone rang. It was word off the ticker that Shastri had died. Viewed from a long way off, he seemed to me to have died at the top of his life's achievement. The very last pictures of him and Ayub after what seemed a real forward step in the Kashmir dispute. This morning's Post had carried our dinner for him as part of my calendar for the next few weeks. Well, many hours had gone into the list, and we will save it, for likely some Indian chief of State will come over in next few months.

The Central Intelligence Bulletin for 11 January 1966 discussed the Tashkent accord and said that "the sudden death of Prime Minister Shastri confronts the Indian leadership with the difficult task of finding a suitable successor at a time when the nation faces grave economic and foreign problems". The same day, there was a Congressional briefing, in the course of which the

CIA representative discussed Shastri's successor and India's stand on nuclear weapons. With regard to the first, the CIA said: "We do not believe, however, that there will be any significant change in Indian policy, domestic or foreign, no matter who is chosen [to be next PM]". Regarding the latter, it was stated that "all of India's major leaders have declared their opposition to a nuclear weapons program and we do not think they will reverse this policy soon".

On 13 January 1966, after Shastri's last rites, the US Vice President Hubert Humphrey and Secretary of State Rusk met Acting Prime Minister Gulzarilal Nanda and others in New Delhi and discussed Tashkent and other issues. "Nanda noted India had made progress despite problems and tensions confronting it; Vice President agreed and said US supported effort at Tashkent and that he had told Kosygin of President Johnson's gratification at the outcome of the Tashkent meeting".

Americans spoke the same language in Pakistan. Their Embassy, on 19 January, sent an account of the US ambassador's talk with President Ayub Khan. The ambassador conveyed America's 'great appreciation for Ayub's high statesmanship in reaching Tashkent agreement' and that the US was following developments stemming from Tashkent 'with interest and sympathy and with a disposition to do everything possible to support and help in conciliatory course he [Ayub] is following.' In response, Ayub said, 'Prime Minister Shastri had realised necessity of peace for both India and Pakistan.' He added that Pakistan's defence minister, who had attended Shastri's funeral, reported that Indians 'seemed relieved to see him' but he did not know how Indian government felt. Ayub told the US ambassador that 'there appeared to be good general reception of Tashkent declaration in India, although no doubt some dissatisfaction was bound to be present on both sides.'

Further records also show that America was satisfied with what happened in Tashkent and praised both Shastri and Ayub. In a meeting with Indian ambassador BK Nehru on 2 February 1966, President Johnson indicated that he was 'terribly proud' of what India did at Tashkent in moving towards reconciliation with Pakistan. 'Shastri died the right way in the cause of peace, not at the end of a gun barrel.' Ambassador Nehru replied that Prime Minister Gandhi had asked him to tell him that 'India was going all-out to make Tashkent work'. On 10 February, Johnson wrote a letter to Ayub Khan. "I have greatly admired what you and Prime Minister Shastri did at Tashkent in the cause of peace", he wrote, adding, "What you and India can do to keep the spirit of Tashkent alive will greatly affect what we as friends of both countries can do to help".

On 22 March 1966, just before Indira Gandhi visited America, Johnson told media persons that he looked forward to discussing with her some of the things he had wanted to discuss 'when I planned to see Prime Minister Shastri and was prevented from doing so by his death. We will take up where we left off there.' Speaking on the lawns of the White House in the presence of Gandhi on 28 March, Johnson welcomed her 'as the leader of our sister democracy.' He said: 'Someone has said that all pleasure is edged with sadness. Only two months ago we looked forward to receiving your gallant predecessor here in our Capital in Washington. We share your grief in his sudden and untimely death.' On 4 May 1966 in a meeting with Indian Planning Minister Ashok Mehta, Johnson reiterated that 'Americans were pleased with Tashkent' and that they 'longed for both India and Pakistan to "bend a little" so that their resources would not be used for war.' He described the Tashkent accord as an 'important achievement' that should be carried forward. He paid tribute to Shastri for 'his efforts with Kosygin to get Hanoi to the peace table.'

After Johnson, Richard Nixon took over as US President in 1969. The recordings of his talks with his top aides are full of foul language he indiscriminately used against anyone and everyone who came in his way, Americans and foreigners alike. In private, Nixon employed profanities to describe Indians and Indira Gandhi. His administration is remembered for its tilt towards Pakistan and lowest point in Indo-US relations. And yet, in a formerly Top Secret backgrounder about Russian premier Kosygin, Nixon's National Security Adviser Henry Kissinger, who shared his world view at that time, wrote that "the sudden fatal heart attack of Indian Prime Minister Shastri at Tashkent has never been traced, by any one, to the effect of his personal encounters with Kosygin".

All of this boils down to a clear conclusion that Americans were warm towards Shastri. They did not think he was going to develop nuclear weapons, or threaten American interests in any way. And they welcomed the Tashkent pact and shared the general positive perception about Kosygin. There is also nothing in the extant records to show that the Americans had any suspicions about Shastri's death, at least in the early period as the news came. Consequently, all the conspiracy theories about Americans having a hand in Shastri's death have nothing to stand on. These theories spouted in an atmosphere marked by deep suspicions against the CIA, due to its activities in some other parts of the world.

In those days of bitter Cold War rivalry, the CIA ruthlessly furthered the American interest, often in direct confrontation with the Soviet KGB. Its inglorious covert operations included the fermenting coups in Iran, Guatemala and the abortive 1961 Bay of Pigs invasion to overthrow Fidel Castro's regime with the assistance of CIA-trained Cuban exiles. Nobody believes that the CIA was created for the welfare of mankind. Neither was R&AW. The CIA remained out of limelight as long as it could, but was eventually dragged into public glare in the 1970s. The unpopularity of Vietnam War, persisting conspiracy theories about the John F Kennedy assassination, accusations of attempted assassinations of foreign leaders and spying on the US citizens turned out to be a prelude to a new era of openness and public oversight of intelligence related matters through the US Congress. The CIA got more bad press after revelations of burglaries of the Watergate complex by ex-CIA agents and President Nixon's misuse of the agency to impede the investigations.

Wary of Nixon's misdeeds, the US Congress began asserting the lawmakers' right to seek oversight of the US Presidency and the executive branch of the US Government. The Hughes-Ryan Act of 1974 was a milestone; it required the President to report all covert operations of the CIA to Congressional committees. Later, an amended Intelligence Oversight Act of 1980 mandated the intelligence agencies to report covert actions to the US Congress.

In 1975, the President's Commission on Central Intelligence Agency activities within the United States or the Rockefeller Commission investigated the CIA's illegal domestic activities. In its final report on 6 June 1975, the Commission found that the CIA had committed unlawful acts within the United States that included infiltrating dissident groups, opening private mail, testing behavior-inducing drugs on unknowing citizens, and subjecting foreign defectors to physical abuse and prolonged confinement. In January 1975, the Senate established the Church Committee. The Church Committee's investigation uncovered allegations such as CIA-led assassination plots against Fidel Castro. The Committee's recommendations made President Gerald Ford issue an Executive Order banning US sanctioned assassinations of foreign leaders. In 1975 only, the House of Representatives established the Pike Committee to investigate illegal domestic activities of government intelligence agencies.

At no point in the course of this long churning process under the media glare was Shastri's name taken even once. The CIA's sabotage and assassination activities were directed at those countries and people who were perceived to be hostile towards America, or who posed a threat to vital American interests. Cuba was not India, and Castro was not Shastri. No American president would welcome the head of Cuban government to the White House; much less hold an umbrella to shelter him from rain.

On 28 February 1966, speaking in the House of Representatives, William Murphy of Illinois spoke of general sense of 'profound shock' felt in his country over 'the sudden death at Tashkent of India's Prime Minister Lal Bahadur Shastri.' He included in the Congressional record the full text of an editorial which appeared in the Gazette of India Extraordinary on 14 January 1966 in remembrance of Shastri. 'All the world joins the people of India in mourning the passing of this great statesman,' said Murphy, summing up the feeling in America over India's misfortune.

NINE
Soviet hand or Indian?

WITH THE ALLEGATION of an American hand in the Shastri death mystery proven baseless, the conspiracy theory linking the Soviet Union to the tragedy needs to be explored. At first thought, the idea is revolting. How can one even imagine such a thing about a country that's traditionally been India's most reliable strategic ally? If Americans had no reasons to remove Shastri from the stage, what could have been the motive for the Soviets with whom we've had far more cordial relations, even in those days? True that the Soviet Union was a totalitarian state, but which regime would want to assassinate the leader of a friendly nation of the size and importance of India? That too on its own territory, soon after an international conference that ended the way it desired? What benefits were the Soviets to derive from such a hideous crime?

Given that Shastri died on the territory of the Soviet Union and there are doubts and suspicions, the narrative needs to go forward from where we left it in chapters 3 and 4. There was a war of tabloids following the discovery of the fake Shastri letter and, the case against the Soviet Union as made by *March of the Nation* and *Current,* was elaborated by Dahyabhai V Patel in his 1970 booklet *Was Shastri Murdered*? Dahyabhai did not mention anywhere in it nor did he otherwise reveal in his public life (in deference to the command of his father not to use his name) that he was Sardar Vallabhbhai Patel's son.

Dahyabhai made no bones about his deep suspicion that the Soviets were involved somehow. He bluntly asked: 'If the conclusion to be drawn from the printing of the Shastri letter forgery in *Blitz* is that the Russians murdered Shastri, the question naturally arises, why?' We now know that it was not the KGB but the CIA which forged the letter. Patel died in 1973, long before Walter McIntosh, the CIA officer who crafted the letter, owned up his act. But even if this had emerged in his lifetime, Patel wouldn't have changed his stand because even McIntosh himself feared that his agency might have unwittingly assisted the KGB in carrying out the assassination of Shastri. In Dahyabhai Patel's estimate, the very background of the Tashkent conference provided a "sufficient reason to liquidate Shastri". And that for "one limb of the Soviet government at least" there was a reason "important enough to outweigh every other consideration". During the long months the Tashkent preliminaries dragged on, he wrote, "it became fairly obvious that Premier Kosygin was desperately eager to act as a mediator between India and Pakistan and to bring about a settlement between the two neighbours that had defied the best efforts of Britain and the United States".

Dahyabhai underlined that "it is also well known that even when the conference finally got under way both India and Pakistan were intensely suspicious of each other and that their leaders wrangled for several days and appeared to have arrived at a complete deadlock before Kosygin's last-minute pressure brought them together to sign the Declaration". He cited the *Blitz's* coverage to substantiate his point. The pro-Soviet tabloid, which persistently plugged the Tashkent Conference, was quite open about the magnitude of the Soviet stakes involved. Its reports from Tashkent were full of lavish praise for the Soviets achieving what America and Britain had failed to achieve—bringing India and Pakistan together. In one report, *Blitz* hailed Kosygin as the world's leading statesman. "By this one stroke of diplomacy you have established yourself in the front rank of the world leaders of today. No bouquet we can offer can match the praise you deserve".

Patel summarised that the Tashkent conference was a matter of prestige and great consequence both to Kosygin and to the Soviet Union. "If Tashkent succeeded the Soviets would establish their right to be 'international brokers'. And if Tashkent failed, then both the Soviet Union and Kosygin would be the subject of ridicule from Western Powers who would deride them as upstarts who had tried to engage in a diplomatic exercise for which they lacked both experience and aptitude and had deservedly made fools of themselves". Patel continued that there was plenty of material in the public domain to indicate that Shastri "had been pushed by Kosygin into signing the Declaration", and that Shastri "was seriously perturbed about having given way to Premier Kosygin's pressure".

"Even while the Tashkent conference was in the planning stage it would not have required any great political acumen to predict that a very strong body of public opinion in India was certain to be totally opposed to any concessions to Pakistan, which it would consider in effect a sell-out, particularly after the recent Indo-Pak hostilities had ended, in the common view, in India's favour. The extensive Soviet news-gathering mechanism in India, which is run in close co-ordination with the diplomatic wing and is even formally a part of the

Soviet embassy, would assuredly have known the extent of the opposition in India at the time to the very idea of holding a Conference. In such an atmosphere, anybody with a crucial stake in ensuring that Tashkent was a success would realise that it was entirely possible that even if Shastri was bulldozed by Kosygin into signing an Agreement, political pressures after his return to India might well induce Lal Bahadur to go back on it, or at least water it down This would assuredly have entailed disastrous loss of face for Kosygin's first major assay in international diplomacy".

Menacingly, Patel then wrote that there was however one way to ensure that Indian public opinion would accept the Tashkent declaration:

> If Shastri died immediately after signing the Declaration, there would be such a strong emotional groundswell in his favour that it would effectively neutralise any conceivable opposition. The Tashkent Accord would, in effect, be considered Shastri's last public act before his 'martyrdom' in the cause of peace, and the upsurge of loyal sentiment to the 'martyr' would outweigh any possible political factors and bring Indian public opinion round to accepting Tashkent and, incidentally, enable the Soviet Union to achieve a major diplomatic triumph in a field hitherto a monopoly of the West.

The thought is utterly scary because the deftness with which Patel articulated it would make it appear plausible to many. More so, if it is read along with an insider's account provided by senior journalist Prem Prakash earlier this year. With India refusing to cede any territory in Kashmir, 'we could clearly see the pressure that the Soviet Union was putting on India to relent,' the ANI chairman recalled. He remembered Alexei Kosygin arriving at Shashtriji's dacha and asking Swaran Singh to get the agreement signed. Swaran Singh replied some words to the effect "how can I impose my opinion on him, he decides". Kosygin left after a while—disappointed.

> A day later, we knew that the talks had failed. Shastriji was willing to vacate mainland Pakistani areas that India had captured, but was not willing to vacate any territory of Kashmir retaken by India. Jammu and Kashmir was an integral part of India. Pakistan wanted the strategic Haji Pir back along with other areas lost by it. The Indian Army was firmly against Haji Pir being ceded as it is the route from where infiltration takes place into Kashmir. With Shastriji unwilling to concede and pressure mounting on him, the Indian delegation announced that it was going back. On 10th January, we all went out for shopping as talks had been abandoned and the next day

we were scheduled to fly out. Suddenly hordes of Soviet information officials came rushing to the market areas to announce that an accord was to be signed and asked all of us to get back to the venue. None of us could believe what had happened in the intervening period. What were the pressures worked on India? The Tashkent Accord was concluded—India had ceded the Haji Pir Pass along with all other territories it had captured. A victory was now turned into status quo ante. What were the pressures put on the Prime Minister of India that claimed his life? Was it the Soviet Union's ploy to win Pakistan away from the United States in its Cold War that killed Shastriji? Who were the mandarins at the Foreign Office who carried out the Soviet Union's wishes to pressure the Prime Minister to sign?[1]

One can even read much into declassified American records[2] to go with Patel's hypothesis. The Central

1 **"Come down your Prime Minister is dead"—A first hand account of the night PM Shastri Died**. Accessed from https://www.aninews.in/news/national/general-news/come-down-your-prime-minister-is-dead-a-first-hand-account-of-the-night-pm-shastri-died201801111841140001/.

2 CIA's records can be accessed from the agency's Electronic Reading Room: https://www.cia.gov/library/readingroom/home

State Department records can be accessed from the Office of the Historian website: https://history.state.gov/.

Intelligence Bulletin on 28 December 1965 commented that the Soviets harboured "no illusions that the Tashkent meeting will bring any basic Indian-Pakistani accommodation" but just hoped that "the summit talks will improve the atmosphere" and foil Chinese gameplan to gain influence. In his letter to Johnson from Tashkent on 6 January, Shastri himself disclosed that the talks were "facing many difficult issues". CIA's assessment on 11 January 1966 was that "the Tashkent declaration signed yesterday by President Ayub and the late Prime Minister Shastri went beyond what either side seemed prepared to concede a week ago".

> The Indians had previously refused to vacate the posts they captured in northern Kashmir without firm guarantees against renewed Pakistani infiltrations. The Indian concession on this point, which may come under heavy fire from hardliners in New Delhi, is probably the result of persistent Soviet encouragement.

Consequently, in the CIA's view, "Premier Kosygin can return to Moscow satisfied that he has achieved the limited objectives the USSR had hoped for in convening the meeting". On 13 January, when US Vice President and Secretary of State met with Prime Minister Nanda and others, LK Jha, Secretary to the PM, gave an account of the talks in Tashkent. He said Shastri indicated a willingness to agree to almost anything but said "he could not return to India without something he could show as a gain". By 8 January there was a "complete breakdown" in the talks. According to Jha, until this point Kosygin had confined his activities to exploring the ground privately and separately with Shastri and Ayub but had made no proposal of his own. Then, starting at 9:00 in the morning on 9 January and continuing until 12:30 next morning, Kosygin went back and forth, working from his own draft of communiqué.

"From Indian point of view language was acceptable as reiteration of well known position. On ceasefire, Pakistan first tried to confine language to commitment to observe ceasefire along ceasefire line; Shastri said this did not go far enough in covering problem of infiltrators, and result was obligation to observe terms of ceasefire on ceasefire line. Hardest decision of all for Shastri was to accept this as adequate assurance on which to base agreement to withdraw from Haji Pir Pass."

On19 January, Ayub Khan told the US Ambassador that "Russians were helpful in moving Indians along in reasonable direction". He said Kosygin worked night and day at Tashkent and Russians played a big role in making the Tashkent agreement agreeable to both nations. The CIA weekly summary for 21 January made a clear observation that Shastri's death gave the Tashkent agreement "a certain sanctity in India".

The US records thus support some of Patel's contentions. But at the same time, they also make it clear that there was no foul play. They laud Kosygin's leadership. We also have to think back to Lalita Shastri's impression towards the end of her 1970 interview with *Dharmyug*. She said knowing her husband, he was "by nature not amenable to pressure, not even that of Pandit ji". And if he "agreed to any compromise, it must be out of conviction that it was in the interests of his country and not under any pressure". She also made it clear that "as far as the question about suspicions about the Russians and their leaders are concerned, I may say that Shri Kosygin is a very good man". She pressed that it made no sense for "any country to kill the leader of another friendly country after inviting him there".

Patel, who was obviously aware of Lalita's views, was not in entire disagreement with this line of thinking. He clarified in his booklet that his postulation by no means implied that "either the Russian government or Premier Kosygin was privy to the Shastri murder".

> The liquidation of the Prime Minister of a friendly nation, planned as a trump card to ensure the success of a difficult diplomatic enterprise, is something too horrendous ever to have obtained official sanction. It would emphatically not have been countenanced by Kosygin, a technocrat whose orderly mind would be completely alien to such intricate and devious manoeuvres. But the men who plotted the assassination would belong to a different discipline altogether—to the Secret Services, in which decency and the laws of hospitality are easily expendable if the cause is pressing enough.

Building up his theory on the basis of what was reported in *March of the Nation* earlier, Patel foisted the blame on the KGB. There have been a number of fully-documented instances in the past, he elucidated, where the KGB and its forerunners under various names, operated without the authority and behind the back of the Government. "That the OGPU and NKVD 'Murder Bureaux' worked overtime in the Stalin era is no longer in doubt". But "State killings did not cease after Stalin's death as commonly believed; they simply went underground".

Patel cited two examples. He recalled the time when Soviet Premier Nikita Khrushchev was working for a rapprochement with West Germany. Chancellor Ludwig

Erhard was scheduled to visit the Soviet Union. In September 1964, Horst Schwirkmann, a German embassy specialist in detecting and countering wiretaps and similar apparatus, was shot in the buttocks with a nitrogen-based mustard gas capsule while touring a religious site outside Moscow. Angered, the Germans almost called off the summit before Khrushchev publicly apologised in time.

> This episode makes it fairly obvious that the man who tried to liquidate the German electronics expert did so over Khrushchev's head and solely on orders from the KGB which, although nominally an arm of the Soviet government, operates in effect as an autonomous "invisible government". This is particularly true of the Mokryye Dela, the "Department of Dirty Tricks" or "wet business", "wet" in the sense of blood. The section that handles these undercover deals is one of the most powerful directorates of the KGB.
>
> Whether by coincidence or because he publicly admitted Soviet guilt in the attack against Schwirkmann, two days after he "apologized" to the West Germans, Premier Khrushchev was toppled from power. In the light of this incident it is entirely possible that the KGB, in the misguided but completely sincere belief that it would be ensuring success for the Tashkent Conference for which

> Kosygin had striven so hard, quietly eliminated Shastri in order to create a "martyr" who would counter any hostile reactions.

The second example given by Patel pertained to the murder in Munich of two Ukrainan political émigré leaders Lev Rebet and Stepan Bandera in 1957 and 1959. Both were deemed to have died of natural causes till a KGB agent defected to West Germany in 1961. Bogdan Stashinsky told American authorities during interrogation that it was he who had assassinated both the leaders using a weapon which fired poisonous liquid on his victims' faces. Thereafter, the German police reopened the cases and found evidence to corroborate Stashinsky's shocking claim. They exhumed Rebet's body and discovered that he had not died of a coronary attack, but had been poisoned as Stashinsky confessed. Stashinsky was then duly tried, convicted and sentenced.

To Patel, the Stashinsky affair had a "particular bearing" on the Shastri case. "Stashinsky murdered Rebet by squirting him with cyanide. But though the Germans can hardly be accused of technological backwardness, the post-mortem that was conducted on Rebet's body revealed nothing out of the ordinary and the police accepted it as a normal case of heart failure". He further reasoned that motive was not enough to pinpoint guilt of murder, there had to be an opportunity as well. In his view, the KGB had it because its men guarded the dacha where Shastri was put up. "They had ample opportunity of murdering Shastri either by administering poison in the glass of milk he was in the habit of taking when he retired, or by introducing in his drinking water a drug that would cause a partial collapse and then finishing him off by means of an injection given under pretext of administering first aid".

> This is not quite as fantastic as might appear. Mrs Lalita Shastri, the late Prime Minister's widow, has recently revealed that when members of his party finally arrived on the scene after his collapse, Lal Bahadur kept pointing at the glass of water (presumably filled from his own flask) yet refused to touch the glass when it was handed to him. At the very least this indicates that Shastri believed the water had been poisoned. It is significant—extremely significant—that the flask from which the glass was filled has disappeared.

To Patel's mind, it was relatively safe for the KGB to use poison because Shastri was already a heart patient. "A heart attack could quite logically be cited as the cause of his death, corroborative evidence could be provided by blaming the stresses and strains of the Tashkent conference, an autopsy could be vetoed as 'desecration of the body of a great man'." Had Shastri's death been natural, there was no reason for the body to bear cuts on the back of the neck and on the stomach.

> The presence of these cuts is impossible to explain except on the assumption that some form of post-mortem examination was carried out or was at least planned. An autopsy would, of course, require incisions of this kind to be made. One can only assume that it was a Soviet doctor who made these cuts, but that after the initial incisions were made, there was a sudden change of mind and, perhaps under orders from somebody higher up, no further examination was carried out and the cuts were concealed with surgical tape. Certainly Dr Chugh cannot have made them and yet have kept silent after the recent outcries on the subject.

The case that Dahyabhai Patel thus made against the KGB was, yet again, not devoid of facts in so far as particular incidents cited by him were concerned. Like other intelligence agencies, the KGB did target those considered hostile by Moscow. Indeed it was possible for an intelligence agency of a major country even in those days to have murdered someone and yet make it look like a natural death. A 1964 estimate by the CIA noted that the KGB resorted to murder to combat potential threats to the Soviet regime. There were techniques involving the use of poison "because murders can be accomplished more surreptitiously in this manner and in some instances without leaving easily recognizable traces of foul play". The CIA record referred to Stashinskiy's targeting the Ukrainian leaders by shooting liquid poison into their faces.

> The effect of the poisonous vapours is such that the arteries which feed blood to the brain become paralysed almost immediately. Absence of blood in the brain precipitates a normal paralysis of the brain or a heart attack, as a result of which the victim dies. The victim is clinically dead within one and one-half minutes after inhaling these poisonous vapours. After about five minutes the effect of the poison wears off entirely, permitting the arteries to return to their normal condition, leaving no trace of the killing agent which precipitated the paralysis or the heart attack. Allegedly, no foreign matter can be discovered in the body or on the clothes of the victim, no matter how thorough an autopsy or examination.

That's that, but, howsoever plausible it may seem, the scenario projected by Dahyabhai Patel is too much of a stretch in my view. The people targeted by the Soviets as cited by Patel were not in the league of Shastri. There is always a method in the madness. It is one thing to quietly target a rebel in a foreign land while he is walking around alone. It is not quite the same thing to even think of it when one is the head of a government of a big, friendly country. He's your guest, is kindly disposed towards you, is accompanied by a big delegation and personal staff, and is being constantly followed by journalists from all over the world. If the attempt fails, or even if it succeeds, and the word gets out, your relations with the friendly country would be scarred forever.

At the same time, assuming Patel's suspicions were correct, the last thing the KGB would have done was to round up, on suspicions of poisoning, Ahmed Sattarov, Mohammed Jan and others who had prepared Shastri's last dinner. They would have on the contrary done everything to cover their tracks, give no hint whatsoever there was anything more to Shastri's death than a heart attack. But not only were the cooks rounded up by them, the Russians also offered to carry out a post-mortem on Shastriji's body—a clear proof of their bona fides. LP Singh, the Home Secretary in January 1966, himself let this out, probably mistakenly, in his 1996 book *Portrait of Lal Bahadur Shastri: A Quintessential Gandhian* (Ravi Dayal Publisher, New Delhi). Though his intent was to dispel conspiracy theories, Singh ended up furnishing another reason to question the official account, which spoke of no such offer. This was despite allegations in Parliament by MP Bhargava of the ruling party that Russians wanted a post-mortem "because they themselves probably suspected some foul play".

LP Singh disclosed that Soviet authorities had actually informed Ambassador TN Kaul of their desire to carry out a post-mortem as "it was the practice in the Soviet Union to conduct a post-mortem examination of the body of a high functionary". What Singh did not know was that autopsies were also performed in the Soviet Union if poisoning was suspected—which was clearly the case in this instance going by what happened to Ahmed Sattarov and other cooks. A CIA report from November 1952 states that even in the crueller times of Joseph Stalin "despite the low regard put to one's life in the USSR, extreme care is taken to ascertain the cause of death in each individual case". This was "particularly true in the case of suspected poisoning, accidental deaths and murder". The record, declassified in 2014, elaborated that "where there is a suspicion of poisoning, a complete chemical examination is made of all organs. In many instances it is necessary to send the organs to a bacteriological institute for examination".

But the Russian offer was declined by India. Kaul consulted Singh, who told him that 'In India a post-mortem was generally considered something bordering on defilement of a dead body.' Going by his account, Singh took this decision in Tashkent keeping in mind Shastri's medical history and circumstances leading to his death which were consistent with a heart attack. He thought a post-mortem was "wholly uncalled for". But how is it that Singh did not know of the Russian suspicions, which led to TN Kaul's cook's arrest? Kaul must have been aware of it. Did he not share this shocking information with the Foreign and Home Secretaries and the Ministers? There is nothing to show that he did. Why? Why would India's ambassador hide such an explosive information concerning the death of the Prime Minister? Why would he go on to pressurise Kuldip Nayar to issue statement against charges of poisoning? Why would he never publicly discuss the Shastri death matter when he was clearly a person who believed in discussing past events indiscreetly?

So, if Americans had nothing to do with Shastri's death and Russians most likely had no hand either, who else could have triggered Shastri's death in Tashkent? In the age of social media, the most scandalous among the Lal Bahadur Shastri death conspiracy theories has come to be discussed more openly than ever before. In the course of a heated exchange with the chair in the Rajya Sabha on 18 December 1970, Raj Narain dragged Indira Gandhi's name to the controversy, openly alleging that she might have something to do with what happened in Tashkent. He said that all over the country people were saying that Shastri had been killed at the behest of those who wanted her to become Prime Minister. He said Indira Gandhi's name appeared on top in this connection because—in Raj Narain's words—she used to lament that her "household servant" became prime minister while she could not.

वह हमारे घर का नौकर प्रधान मंत्री बन गया और मै ऐसे ही रह गई।

Narain alleged that Indira did not even want to join Shastri's government. 'One day Shastri said if you want to join, come and hold Information and Broadcasting portfolio, but nothing more you will get.' When the chair asked him what was he driving at, Narain pulled into the controversy a flamboyant, disreputable character whose name is taken in the same breath as that of Vijay Mallya, Lalit Modi and Nirav Modi. This is what Narain said in the House about Jayanti Dharma Teja:

> He is reported to have said that my name has been taken in the matter over the death of Lal Bahadur Shastri, so it is risky for me to return to India. He said I know many things about him. It was I who for the first time in this House had earlier asked whether Dharma Teja was there in Tashkent or not. [Home Minister] Chavan said there was some other Teja. …I want to know from Home Minister whether he has any information about Teja's relationship with Prime Minister Shastri? Is the Government aware that Teja wanted to meet him but Shastri had blocked his access?

A vivid portrayal of Dharma Teja appears in a remarkable book written after the lifting of Emergency by Janardan Thakur—a top most political correspondent of the 1970s. *All the Prime Minister's Men* (Vikas Publishing House, Delhi) is about colourful and controversial people close to India's first family. Teja was the "smoothest of operators" among them according to Janardan Thakur. He became a "courtier" at the Teen Murti House in the days of Pandit Nehru. He would always be accompanied by "his gorgeous wife, Ranjit Kaur, whom he had married after the mysterious death of his first wife, a rich American

Jewess, in a Rome hotel".[3]

A nuclear physicist whose 1959 thesis had been uploaded on the website of CERN, Teja overnight turned into a shipping tycoon. In 1961, he started a company with an initial capital of Rs 200 and wangled a loan of Rs 20 crores from the Government of India. "Kuchh thoda sa de do" (give him a little something) was all that the gracious Nehru had told his minister—as per *All the Prime Minister's Men*. According to an article by renowned journalist Inder Malhotra on *Rediff.com*[4] some bureaucrats, particularly in the Directorate General of Shipping, had deep reservations and that's why the matter was referred to the Cabinet. Rupees twenty crores is "chickenfeed today but was an astronomical sum 54 years ago", read an article in the digital newspaper *The News Minute* in June 2015. Answering a question in Parliament in March 1962, the Government stated that "from such information as we have gathered, it appeared that Shri JD Teja is a very enterprising businessman" and the "main consideration which influenced the Government" in giving him the loan

---

3 "The story of his wife's death in a hotel in Rome sometime in 1960-61, has been the subject of unsavoury gossip," commented an article in *The Illustrated Weekly* of India in 1971.

4 Inder Malhotra, **Before Ramalinga Raju, there was Dharma Teja**, 12 February 2009. Accessed from: http://www.rediff.com/money/2009/feb/12-before-raju-there-was-dharma-teja.htm.

was that "no risk was involved to the Government and the advantages that would accrue to India were considerable".

Thus Teja rocketed into fame in the Nehruvian era. He came to possess offices and luxury apartments in New York, London, Paris, Rome and the French Riviera. Amongst his "chums" in Delhi were TN Kaul, and Nehru's cousin RK Nehru (Ambassador to US). Thakur writes that Kaul loved photography, and so whenever Teja went and stayed with him in Moscow, he would take him some latest model of a film projector or a camera. "For some he brought electronic gadgets, for some mechanical toys, and for yet others the most expensive mink coats". *The News Minute* story reads that Teja "became very close to Indira [after] reportedly presenting her with a mink coat".[5]

Thakur underlined the importance of Teja's second wife in his life in these words: "The beautiful lady was a tremendous asset for her husband. She was a great success, and not just with bankers and business magnates. She could turn on many an old politician".

At Teen Murti, the Tejas would be in their element. They never missed a chance to please the Nehru-

5 **Meet Jayanti Dharam Teja, the Lalit Modi of the 60's, 19 June 2015**. Accessed from: https://www.thenewsminute.com/article/meet-jayanti-dharam-teja-lalit-modi-60s.

Gandhis—including young Sanjay and Rajiv. Thakur's book suggests that Teja was something of a guardian to them when they were abroad. "Any time they needed money, they had just to ask 'Uncle Teja'."

By all accounts, Teja's dream run came to an end in 1964. *All the Prime Minister's Men* reads:

> The Tejas had managed the Nehrus, but their charm did not work with that little man who succeeded Jawaharlal. One day, when Teja was summoned by Lal Bahadur Shastri, he had turned up with his wife. Shastri did not like it, and told Teja curtly, 'The appointment was for you, not for your wife.'

Claims made a few years later in Parliament by Opposition MPs (not fully negated by the Government) had it that Shastri obtained a written statement from G Narayana, nephew of Teja and a director in his company, about the irregularities. The Shastri government initiated legal action against Teja. But after Shastri passed away, Teja got back to the big league. In Washington, DC to cover Prime Minister Indira Gandhi's official visit to the US in March 1966, Inder Malhotra bumped into Teja at a dinner at the home of G Parathasarathi, India's Ambassador to the United Nations at that time.

The wheel of law was turning in the meanwhile. Fearing that he would be arrested, in June 1966 Teja made good his escape from a 5-star hotel in Delhi. Nabbed a year later in New York, he jumped a bail of 20,000 dollars and flew off to Costa Rica. In July 1970, he was arrested yet again at Heathrow airport in London. In the wake of persistent demands from Opposition leaders, Teja was ultimately brought back to India in April 1971 after incurring a lot of expense[6] in an extradition battle in a London court. An *India Today* special report notes that during the hearing of India's extradition plea in the court, Teja, through his counsel Lord Dingle Foot (former Solicitor General and British MP) claimed that he (Teja) "did diplomatic work for India by running secret missions to the Soviet Union at the time of the Chinese aggression" and "was considered for an ambassadorial posting in the US".[7]

Teja was put on trial, and sentenced to three years' imprisonment in October 1972 for forgery and falsification of the accounts of Jayanti Shipping Corporation. The

---

6 In June, the Ministry of External Affairs informed the Rajya Sabha that "an amount of Rs. 6,66,000 has been incurred so far on the arrest and extradition of Dr Dharma Teja to India. Bills towards fees of solicitors and counsels amounting to Rs. 2,98,400 are pending for payment with the High Commission of India, London".

7 Sumit Mitra, **Jayanti Dharma Teja: An unheralded comeback**, *India Today*, 24 July 2013.

India Today report reads that Teja also contravened the Passport Act, which debars anyone convicted for more than two years from acquiring a passport for five years from the date of conviction. "Yet Teja not only acquired a passport, he had made one trip out of the country in May 1977, a full five months before the restriction ran out".[8]

Teja's 1977 "escape" led to much commotion in Parliament and outside. Prime Minister Morarji Desai apparently had a good view of him, but his successor Charan Singh did not. His short-lived government filed a suit against Pan American, the airline which had flown Teja out of the country. As the cases dragged on, Teja renewed his passport three times in Geneva. "And as the years wore on, he renewed old contacts: in 1981, he met Prime Minister Indira Gandhi, an old family friend, and flew to New York to meet her and son Rajiv Gandhi during their state visit to the US in July 1982",[9] reported *India Today*.

After living abroad for five years, Teja unconcernedly returned to India in February 1983. Journalist SK Aggarwal remarked in his 1989 book *Media Credibility* (Mittal Publications, New Delhi) that he was unmindful

8 Ibid.
9 Ibid.

of "income tax officials still after him, and their claims of unpaid dues having burgeoned to Rs. 13.53 crores by then. Teja not only waived aside the claims but resumed his contacts in high places. Till the end his position remained ambiguous for he still proclaimed innocence".

Inder Malhotra wrote that Ram Manohar Lohia, the principal Nehru-baiter, demanded in Lok Sabha as to what was Teja doing at Tashkent during the India-Pakistan talks. Minister of External Affairs Swaran Singh responded that it was a case of mistaken identity. 'There was a Teja at Tashkent but he is a Foreign Service officer, JS Teja, posted to our Embassy in Moscow.'[10]

Following Raj Narain broadside in Rajya Sabha in December 1970, Deputy Home Minister Ram Niwas Mirdha stood up to clarify, as Swaran Singh had done in the Lok Sabha, that it was IFS officer Dr JS Teja who was present in Tashkent not Dr Dharma Teja 'about whom prosecution is going on.'[11] Raj Narain snapped: Was Dharma Teja in Moscow or not? The Minister replied: He was not in Tashkent. Narain repeated his question whether or not Dharma Teja was in Soviet Russia at the

---

10 Inder Malhotra, **Before Ramalinga Raju, there was Dharma Teja**, 12 February 2009. Accessed from: http://www.rediff.com/money/2009/feb/12-before-raju-there-was-dharma-teja.htm.

11 Dr JS Teja rose to be as India's Permanent Representative to the UN offices in Geneva in 1986.

time of Shasri's death? Mirdha again answered that as per information available to him, Dharma Teja was not in Tashkent and he had no connection with this matter.

After some time, LK Advani joined the issue: 'A reference to Mr Jayanti Teja was made just now and the honourable Minister tried to say that Mr Teja was nowhere near Tashkent at that time. I would like to know from him specifically whether it is not a fact that on December 23, 1965, Jayanti Teja emplaned from Bombay for Moscow and was in Moscow from December 23 to December 28, and that he stayed with the Ambassador Mr Kaul there. And December 23-28, 1965, was just a few days before Shastriji's death took place at Tashkent. So it cannot be said that what Jayanti Teja is saying in the London court has nothing to do with his presence in Moscow.'

Mirdha replied that he was going to stick to his statement that 'so far as we know Teja was not in Tashkent in those days...You said he was in Moscow. Sir, this is most irrelevant.'

And this is where this particular trail ended. This was all that there was to the alleged link between whatever happened in Tashkent and Indira Gandhi. It did not prove anything, but sparked off speculations that Indira might be "involved". These speculations continue till date and essentially stand on two postulations. One, Indira

Gandhi was hostile towards Lal Bahadur Shastri. Two, her becoming PM soon after Shastri's death was not a coincidence because she was more acceptable to the Soviets as Prime Minister than the former.

With regard to the relations between Shastri and Indira, the two people whose views I am going to go by are late eminent journalists, Kuldip Nayar and Inder Malhotra. Nayar was Shastri's press advisor and Malhotra Indira's biographer. Both had a ringside view of what was happening in political circles since the 1950s. I cherish meeting Malhotra (a former *Times of India* editor who died in 2016) many years ago—but this was in the context of my research about Subhas Chandra Bose. With Nayar, I got lucky earlier this year when I accompanied *The Tashkent Files* unit to his residence. Vivek Agnihotri wanted to record an interview with him, to get his insights about the Shastri matter—more so because he was at that time our only living link to the tragedy in 1966 and subsequent events. Nayar passed away in August 2018.The only living eminent journalist who was present in Tashkent is ANI Chairman Prem Prakash).

At 95, Nayar's mind was nimble and his voice robust. He spoke authoritatively and his recollections were full of wisdom garnered across the decades in places and positions as varied as India House in London, where he was the High Commissioner, and Sansad Bhawan in New

Delhi, where he was an MP. In response to questions by Agnihotri and myself, Nayar spoke on camera about his suspicions about the conduct of TN Kaul. Thereafter in a free-wheeling discussion with Shastri's grandson, Sanjay Nath Singh and I, he remembered other things. Like Indira Gandhi's visit to 10 Janpath after Shastri's death while she was looking for suitable official residence for herself. She wasn't much impressed with Shastri's lifestyle and disparagingly characterised it as "middle class". Nayar also said that Indira was not keen to have a memorial for Shastri at Vijay Ghat—till such time Lalita Shastri threatened that she would sit on a dharna.

In his last and most well-known book, *Beyond the Lines* (Roli Books, Delhi) Kuldip Nayar discussed the issue of Shastri's death and also his equations with Indira Gandhi. He revealed that tension began building up in the days of Nehru itself, when Shastri was No 2. Shastri felt he was being sidelined because Indira harboured some hostility towards him.[12] He even toyed with quitting politics as he thought Nehru had his daughter in his mind

---

12 When celebrated author Ved Meha interviewed Indira Gandhi for his 1970 book *Portrait of India*, she did not hide her disapproval of Shastri. She told Mehta that Shastri "didn't have a modern mind as "he was an orthodox Hindu", adding, "You cannot lead country out of poverty with superstition. You need a modern, scientific mind outlook for that." It is quite well-known that in later years Indira became quite interested in tantric rituals. Shastri is not known to have any interest in such practices.

as his successor. When Nayar told him that there was an impression that he (Shastri) was so devoted to Nehru that he might propose her name after Nehru's death, Shastri replied that he was 'not that much of a sadhu.'

In an essay titled "What if Shastri hadn't died suddenly in Tashkent?" in *Outlook* magazine in 2004, Inder Malhotra opined that in case Shastri had lived on, Indira might never have become prime minister. On the last day of 1965—two days before leaving for Tashkent—Shastri neatly eased out TT Krishnamachari, Finance Minister in his cabinet as he had been in Nehru's. Indira, who regarded Krishnamachari as a friend, was enraged. 'I would be the next to be thrown out,' she angrily told Malhotra.

Malhotra commented that by the time Shastri left for Tashkent, "it was widely known that Indira Gandhi's relations with the prime minister had soured to the point of breaking down". There was a certain complexity in their relationship not likely to be understood by those who did not know them as well as Malhotra did. An assessment by the CIA on 26 June 1964 that while Indira "is said to have favoured delay in choosing a prime minister [after her father's death], there appears to be nothing in her long personal relationship with Shastri or in her views on problems facing the government to keep them from working together" failed to take into account this complexity. In *Outlook*, Malhotra lucidly observed:

> He [Shastri] knew that her presence in the cabinet would give it strength. But he did not want a potential rival in his team. Towards this end, he adopted a dual policy of showing Indira all courtesies and nominating her to the important committees of the cabinet but giving her little real say in the making of high policy. She saw through it all and reacted with a mixture of resentment and defiance.[13]

Malhotra referred to intimate personal letters Indira wrote to a close friend, American writer and photographer Dorothy Norman, between 1950 and 1984. Following Indira's assassination, Dorothy made them public through her book *Indira Gandhi: Letters to An American Friend*. And so it was revealed that "by December 1965, Indira was tired of being an inconsequential member of the cabinet". She wanted to resign and go to London to live there. Rajiv was then at Cambridge and Sanjay at the Rolls-Royce factory at Crewe.[14] By a quirk of irony, Malhotra wrote,

13 Inder Malhotra, **What If Shastri Hadn't Died Suddenly In Tashkent?** *Outlook*, 23 August 2004.

14 Janardan Thakur wrote in **All the Prime Minister's Men** that "finding the wayward boy at a loose end, bent on doing nothing but tinkering with cars and two wheelers, the Tejas offered to take him [Sanjay] with them to England and have him attached to the Rolls Royce factory".

Shastri's mind was also working in the same direction.

> Whether Indira knew it or not—I have a sharp suspicion that she did—he was planning, as he told only a few of his confidants, to offer her the post of High Commissioner to the UK on his return from Tashkent.[15]

The impression that Shastri-Indira relations were frosty[16] thus finds a credible validation. But this is not the case with the idea that her elevation as India's Prime Minister in 1966 was more than a coincidence. The view of conspiracists that Shastri was "removed" with a view to make her PM doesn't stand to scrutiny because

15 Inder Malhotra, **What If Shastri Hadn't Died Suddenly In Tashkent?** *Outlook*, 23 August 2004.

16 Indira Gandhi appears aloof and disinterested in some of the pictures where she is in the same frame as Prime Minister Shastri. There is also an Associated Press reel on YouTube showing her at the Palam airport at the time Shastri's body arrived from Tashkent. The Russians appear crestfallen, but she is stoic. She is seen speaking with someone who appears to be a higher-up and appears to be smirking while speaking to her. But then this cannot be construed to say what conspiracy theories suggest. There is also a picture of Indira's taken in 1976, visiting Vijay Ghat with Lalita Shastri, looking somber. Body language is a tricky thing and I am no expert of it. Fortitude was one of many qualities of Indira Gandhi. She betrayed little emotion even when her son and successor Sanjay was killed in an air crash.

her becoming prime minister was accidental. CIA's intelligence bulletin for 11 January 1966 talked about the efforts to select a successor to Shastri. "Congress Party President Kamaraj has scheduled a meeting of senior party officials for this Friday and a caucus of the party hierarchy will probably follow within the next week or so". It was noted that "among the leading possibilities for the prime ministership" were YB Chavan, Morarji Desai, K Kamaraj, Neelam Sanjiva Reddy and Indira Gandhi. The CIA felt that Reddy and Indira "would become serious contenders for the post only if a deadlock developed among the other candidates". In a Congressional briefing on 11 January, the CIA repeated that "leaders of Congress party face a difficult problem in choosing a successor to Prime Minister Shastri". The leading candidates were Chavan, Desai and Kamraj. Indira topped the list of "dark horses who might be picked up as compromise candidate".

On 21 January, the agency informed US policymakers that "the selection of Mrs Gandhi was largely a matter of political expediency".

> Although officially chosen by secret ballot of the Congress Party's parliamentarians on 19 January, her election was virtually assured some days before when key state and national political leaders rallied behind her as a

> "consensus" candidate. Few of these leaders regarded Indira as their favorite candidate, but they agreed with powerful party president Kamaraj that she was the contender most likely to stop a strong bid by right-wing former finance minister Morarji Desai, a long-standing foe of the "syndicate" of leaders, who brought about Shastri's succession to Nehru. As Nehru's daughter she also enjoys a national image which will be advantageous in the 1967 general elections.

So the conclusion that I draw is that the dots as they appear today cannot be connected to produce a picture to go with the conspiracy theory that Indira Gandhi had something to do with Shastri's death in Tashkent. Because she was not on very good terms with Shastri, and that she was close to Teja who had no particular reason to like Shastri and was probably present in Moscow around the time Shastri died, it doesn't necessarily mean some foul play was enacted at the dacha at her behest. There are so many gaps in this conspiracy theory. Therefore, to level such an outrageous allegation on a foremost national icon, never mind her relations with Shastri, would be sacrilegious to Indira Gandhi's memory. Even so, the events subsequent to Shastri's death do make one thing crystal clear: Indira Gandhi's government held back some vital details regarding the tragedy in Tashkent from the people of India. Therefore, the charge of a cover-up against her over the Shastri case is going to stick, unless something is done to remove it.

TEN

Mega mysteries merged

THE MOST BIZARRE among the conspiracy theories swirling around Lal Bahadur Shastri's death has by some quirk of fate become the most talked about in recent years. It holds that Shastri's death has something to do with the strange case of Subhas Chandra Bose's disappearance, which in turn is India's biggest and longest-running political controversy. Ordinarily, even the most gullible person would have dismissed this outlandish link-up out of hand because, for one, Netaji died long ago in 1945. But extraordinary events of recent years have infused a new life in this theory which was for the first time articulated in public in 1971. Today, included among those who believe that there could be some truth in it are Shastriji's family members and scores of Indians and persons of Indian origin all over the world.

In 2015, when the Subhas Chandra Bose death mystery and related issues started hitting headlines in a big way because of the efforts made by the author and his friends, the Shastri issue also began receiving attention. His surviving sons, Anil and Sunil Shastri and grandsons, Sanjay and Siddharth Nath Singh (children of Shastriji's daughter Suman) made shocking claims. They recalled Shastri's last call from Tashkent to his family that he was not perturbed at all by the criticism over the Tashkent treaty and was actually going to make some big announcement on his return. 'There is a possibility that he wanted to tell the people of India something about Netaji on his return. He was aware of Netaji and we cannot rule out that it had some link with Babuji's mysterious death,' Sunil Shastri told *The Sunday Guardian* on 11 July 2015. Soon, a prominent member of Subhas Bose's family substantiated this account. On August 13, *The Times of India* quoted Netaji's grandnephew, Chandra Kumar Bose, as saying that before leaving for Tashkent, Shastriji told his father Amiya Nath Bose that he would 'search for evidence of Netaji's presence in Russia' during his visit. 'Shastri was serious about it. There is no doubt that he was poisoned. We should find out if it had anything to do with Netaji,' Chandra Bose said.

The Netaji angle theory of Shastriji's death received

a massive boost in December 2015 when, according to *The Times of India*, a Dutch national of Indian origin "produced a forensic face-mapping report by a British expert that has found strong resemblance between Bose and a man photographed with former PM Lal Bahadur Shastri during the Indo-Pak peace talks in Tashkent in 1966". Thereafter, the matter was thrashed out on TV channels in prime time and there were numerous reports and articles in mainstream papers and magazines. This was the closest that the Shastri death controversy came to dominating the headlines for the first time since 1966.

Such a startling backdrop obviously warrants a detailed discussion. To understand and adequately contextualise the sensational claims linking Shastriji to Netaji, it would be essential to first go through a gist of the controversy surrounding Subhas Bose's fate. At a personal level, like in the Netaji matter, my thrust in the Shastriji issue is on bringing about a closure by way of declassification of the official files. We have met with some success in the Netaji case and it is only natural we should seek to replicate it in the case of Shastriji. In the public mind, both these major death controversies of modern India go together. Discussing one invariably leads to the other, as I have personally experienced in the course of my talks about the Netaji issue in universities and other gatherings in India and abroad. Therefore, it makes much sense for those keen to see a closure to the Shastriji matter to acquaint themselves with the basic facts in the Netaji case.

For more than six decades or so, many attempts were made to flag the Netaji issue but never was the country made to sit up and take note of it as in April 2015. It was on the front pages and hotly debated in prime time TV discussions. The reason Netaji and issues related to him still occasionally make it to the news is thanks to what happened in 2015. That year, *India Today* ran a cover story on the basis of certain declassified intelligence files in New Delhi's National Archives that detailed how the Government had spied on the nephews of Netaji for more than two decades after Independence. The real import of the Bose family spying scandal was aptly captured a little later by senior journalist, now Minister of State for External Affairs, MJ Akbar, who said that the 'reasonable explanation for this long surveillance' was that 'the Government was not sure whether Bose was dead, and thought that if he were alive he would be in some form of communication with his family in Calcutta.'

While Congress party's explanation to the ensuing public outrage against its tallest post-Independence leader was that the snooping charge was a result of "motivated news plants, based on selective and mischievous leaks", the reality was quite different. The paper had actually been declassified in the days of Congress's rule itself following spirited efforts made by Chandrachur Ghose and me. Our Right to Information quest compelled the Government to release thousands of pages. These papers reached the National Archives in 2012, and in November 2014 they were opened to researchers. I visited the National Archives in December and spotted the snooping related documents among the released lot. Apparently, they were released by mistake along with other "harmless" records. Without wasting any time, I quickly obtained their copies and then wrote about what I had discovered in my online column in *Swarajya* and then on the *Daily O*, which belongs to the *India Today* group. This was how the top editors at the magazine came to know about the issue. I was contacted and the cover story followed.

A direct outcome of the *India Today* disclosure was that on 17 September the Bengal government released 64 files available with its intelligence branch. Many of them dealt with elaborate surveillance on several of Subhas Bose's kin and freedom fighters. A perusal of these records convinced Chief Minister Mamata Banerjee that Netaji had not died in 1945. In the meanwhile, Narendra Modi government was already in the midst of a massive declassification process. This was the result of lobbying efforts jointly made by Netaji's kin led by Chandra Kumar Bose and a group called "Mission Netaji" formed by this author and friends, including Chandrachur Ghose. My 2012 book *India's Biggest Cover-Up* outlined a blueprint to resolve this matter and declassification was its core element. After the book came out, members of the Bose family came out in support of declassification and we jointly worked towards it.

In October 2015, Modi invited Subhas Bose's kin and others, including "Mission Netaji" members and eminent persons[1] such as Major General GD Bakshi (retd), to his official residence and, in the presence of Home Minister Rajnath Singh and External Affairs Minister Sushma Swaraj, announced his decision to declassify secret Subhas Bose files. This was in full media glare and the biggest story of that time, underlining the considerable public interest. When a bus carrying all of us left for the official residence of the PM, virtually all the media in India followed it, with many channels showing the event live.

The process of declassifying Subhas Bose related files started in January 2016. More than 300 files from the

---

1 Siddharth Nath Singh was also invited as he was then BJP's in-charge for the state of Bengal. It was quite obvious for us to expect similar process for the files relating to Shastriji.

PMO, MHA and MEA have thus far been released, and as per the statement of Prime Minister Modi in January this year, the 'process' is ongoing as other countries are being requested to open their files.

The information available thus far from a variety of sources, including the files released by the Central government as well as in foreign archives, paints a far clearer picture of the Subhas Bose death controversy than ever in history. Similar to the case of Shastri, there is a matrix of three options in the Netaji case. One, the official version that Netaji was killed following an air crash in Taiwan in August 1945, and his remains are deposited at Renkoji temple in Tokyo. Two, he was in USSR after 1945 and was subsequently liquidated as a result of a conspiracy involving Soviet dictator Joseph Stalin and Prime Minister Jawaharlal Nehru. Three, Netaji secretly returned to India and lived in the disguise of a holy man we now call Gumnami Baba in various parts of UP till 1985, when he would have been 88 years old. Many of those who oppose this theory, the most eminent being BJP leader Dr Subramanian Swamy, claim that after Netaji was killed in Soviet Russia, an imposter was planted by the Intelligence Bureau (IB) to misguide the people of India, to prevent them from pursuing Netaji's "killing" in Russia and the role of Pt Nehru. God forbid this should be true!

I personally do not think it is.

In so far as the air crash theory of Netaji's death is concerned, it has been accepted by the Government of India. If this version is correct, the question of Shastriji having to do anything with Netaji in 1966 will not arise. But, in case it can be demonstrated this theory is not correct, or that there are reasonable grounds to question it, then the Government's position will be undermined not only over the Netaji case but also in the Shastriji death matter where the Government has consistently held that there was nothing suspicious about it. If one is found to have lied in one instance, their position would be suspected in other instances as well. I grew up next to a police station in New Delhi. Every time the cops nabbed a thief over one case of theft, he was deemed to be a suspect in other cases of theft in the area. I am sorry to give such an analogy while discussing the conduct of our Government but there are details, more in the Netaji case than in Shastri's, which compel me to draw such an odious analogy.

Subhas Chandra Bose's death occurred when India was ruled by the British. This happened soon after Japan, Netaji's benefactor, decided to surrender to the Allies on 15 August 1945 after having been struck by two nuclear bombs. On 22 August 1945, an announcement was made from the Japanese side that Subhas Bose had died on 18 August following a plane crash in present-day Taipei city in Taiwan A number of Japanese also perished in the reported crash. Most important among whom was Lt General Tsunamasa Shidei—the newly appointed Deputy Chief of Staff (Intelligence) of the Quantung Army, which was preparing to surrender to the Red Army in Manchuria. The crash did not kill everyone on board. Most notable survivor was Bose's ADC Lt Col Habibur Rahman Khan. The Japanese said that Bose was on his way to Tokyo for talks with the Japanese government about the Indian National Army's surrender but the crash ended his journey. Badly burnt, Bose was given treatment in Taipei by army doctors, but died at midnight.

It was the delay in relaying the news of Bose's death by the Japanese and its timing which gave rise to initial suspicions. It would seem to Bose's British foes that "death" had apparently saved him from falling into their hands. Doubts were instantly raised in official circles. "*Bose dead* story not believed in London", read a report in the *Hindustan Times*. "Today's Japanese reports of the death of Subhas Chandra Bose are taken with a grain of salt in circles close to Far Eastern official quarters. …Opinion expressed is that... the timing is too good to be entirely fortuitous".

Contrary to what many would like to think today, doubts about Subhas Bose's fate did not sprout from some fertile Indian mind. 'I suspect it very much; it is just what should be given out if he meant to go underground,' wrote Field Marshal Archibald Wavell, the Viceroy of India, in his personal diary when he heard the news of Bose's death. The first person who publicly claimed to have seen Subhas Bose after his reported death was an American journalist embedded with the US army as it went into Taiwan. Alfred Wagg, then associated with the *Chicago Tribune*, dramatically interrupted a press meet of Jawaharlal Nehru on 29 August 1945 to claim that he had seen Bose near Saigon (now Ho Chi Minh City) a few days after the reported death.

On 1 September, London's *Sunday Observer* picked up Wagg's claim and added that the Japanese report was "not believed in British and American military circles". Wagg went on to repeat his claim in private talks with many top Indian leaders, Gandhi downwards. Mahatma Gandhi's January 1946 statement made headlines the world over. *The New York Times* on 6 January reported Gandhi as declaring in a speech that he "believed Subhas Chandra Bose was still alive and awaiting a propitious time to reappear".

To find out the truth, the authorities started an

inquiry under the lead of the Deputy Director of Intelligence Bureau (IB). W McK Wright was assisted by many of his juniors and army personnel, including IB Assistant Director Phillip Finney and his colleague Bakshi Badrinath, both of whom had been keeping a tab on Bose for long. It did not take McK Wright's team—christened 'Combined Section'—long to discover many loopholes in the Japanese version. For one, the Japanese were lying when they said that Bose was coming over to Tokyo. Finney laid his hands on an interpreter who had attended a secret meeting between Bose and others just before the air crash. Kinji Watanabe arrived to hear his fellow Japanese officers discussing how to get Mr Bose to his destination. 'He was to get to the Russians,' who could have given him refuge at that time.

In his written statement to IB, Watanabe provided further details about Bose's post-war plans. From the very beginning Bose's standpoint was very clear, he underlined. 'He was ever ready to accept any assistance from any nation if only it desired India to be independent.' In the absence of Bose's body or a proper picture of it, the entire story of the death was reconstructed solely on the basis of the verbal eyewitness account of Habibur Rahman, supported by unsatisfactory supporting statements of a few Japanese. It turned out that even Rahman's version was doubtful as his repeated interrogations did not convince the authorities about the veracity of his claims. On 25 March 1946, McK Wright was informed by Colonel GD Anderson, who had supervised Rahman's interrogation at Delhi's Red Fort (which was then the main hub for military and intelligence), that even after months Rahman still 'adhered to his earlier attitude of ingenious denial'. Interrogating officer, Major Hyat Khan, conveyed to Anderson in his report—available in the National Archives in New Delhi—that even if Rahman "was in the know of Bose's plans, he would not disclose them. His manner is not very convincing. He talks in a secretive way even if no one is about".

After he was eventually released in view of the pro-INA feelings across India, Rahman was questioned by Mahatma Gandhi and ace lawyer Sarat Bose, who knew his younger brother Subhas better than anyone else. Gandhi then made a public statement that Rahman had convinced him about the veracity of the Taiwan death theory. But a letter discovered at the Princeton University in America in the 1990s showed that Gandhiji personally did not believe what he said for public consumption. (I'd like to believe that he did so with the intent to keep Bose out of harm's way.) The letter was written in July 1946 on his behalf by his secretary Khurshed Naoroji (granddaughter of Dadabhai Naoroji) to Pulitzer-winning American journalist Louis Fischer, who was pro-India.[2] The Indian army, Fischer was told, had undergone a change and become pro-Russian and even sympathetic to the Indian National Army. 'If Bose comes with the help of Russia, neither Gandhiji nor the Congress will be able to reason with the country,' she emphasised. As for Sarat, he made a public statement months prior to his death in 1950, that so far as he could make out, Rahman 'had orders from his chief to keep his whereabouts a closely guarded secret.' In fact, many believed that Rahman, a Kashmiri who moved to Pakistan after Partition, was just carrying out an order from Bose for his safety.

Further, the intelligence community was confused by reports—including from the Russian sources—that Bose was possibly in Soviet Russia after August 1945. On 9 April 1946, some eight months after Netaji was reported dead, McK Wright's men sat down to ponder over intelligence pooled in from several independent sources. Helping the discussion was a three-page note from the Combined Section summarising the case thus far. It noted at the very start that it was "clear that Bose

2 Fischer's biography of Gandhiji was turned into Oscar-winning biopic by Richard Attenborough in 1980.

and his staff were trying to make a getaway to Russia" and that Rahman and other Bose aides had appeared "to have lied, or withheld their knowledge, about the reasons for the journey which was being made". Inputs received from Congress party sources revealed that Gandhi's claim about Bose being alive was not based on his "inner voice" as he had said, but "secret information which he has received". Most significant was the intelligence gathered from Russian diplomats who were privately talking about a living Subhas Bose in their country.

In May 1946, British intelligence contacted the US Consulate in Bombay. The Americans were told that "the hold which Bose had over the Indian imagination was tremendous, and that if he should return to this country, trouble would result which...would be extremely difficult to quell". The Americans were asked to state their position as they were now in control in Japan and Taiwan. "Positive proof of some kind that Bose is dead would be most interesting", the Consulate wrote to the State Department. The State Department conferred with the War Department and reverted to the Consulate in June 1946: "A search of our files in the Intelligence Division reveals that there is no direct evidence that Subhas Chandra Bose was killed in an airplane crash...despite the public statements of the Japanese to that effect". A shocking aspect of this revelation is that the Government of India in the 1970s accessed copies of these American records, but concealed them from us.

Unable to find any direct evidence of Bose's death and concerned over the reports that he could be in Soviet Russia, the Governments of India and the UK remained non-committal about his death in the 1940s. Declassified minutes of a meeting held at 10 Downing Street under the chairmanship of Prime Minister Clement Attlee on 25 October 1945 noted that "the only civilian renegade of importance" at that time was Subhas Bose.[3] The Japanese "eyewitnesses" were questioned again towards the end of the decade at the behest of the Allied authorities. On 3 October 1946, in the Council of State, Member Ahmed Jaffer asked the Home Member (Minister) Vallabhbhai Patel if the Government of India had any evidence whether Bose was dead or alive. Sardar Patel's response was: 'Government is not in a position to make any authoritative statement on the subject.' However, the situation changed with Prime Minister Jawaharlal Nehru making a statement that very year that he was inclined to believe in the death

---

3 In 1956, when he was in Lucknow on a private visit, Clement Attlee told an inquisitive Chief Minister Dr Sampurnanand that Subhas Bose was in Russia after his reported death. This was overheard by Dharmendra Gaur, a security personnel from the Intelligence Bureau.

of Bose. At the same time, we have on record a note from the Viceroy showing disagreement with the stand taken by Nehru on the basis of what Habibur Rahman had told him. As far as he was concerned, the stand taken by Patel was right. This was the time before 1947 when there was an interim government (led by Nehru) in place.

As the 1940s closed, the controversy about Bose's reported death remained alive as a strong undercurrent. The spectre of his coming back from the dead still troubled those in power. The whispers of his being alive were loud enough to be heard on the other side of the globe by the Central Intelligence Agency. In November 1950, a highly-placed agent in India reported that "it is now currently rumoured in the Delhi area that the 'Netaji', which is Bose's nickname, is alive and is in Siberia, where he is waiting for a chance to make a big comeback".[4]

Despite the Government's position of doubting the news of Subhas Bose's death, in the early 1950s, it was projected by the Nehru regime that he had died and that there was no controversy about it. Nehru was not open to the idea of having the matter probed by a proper inquiry as demanded by so many. Declassified files have notes of

4 I obtained this report from the CIA using the American Freedom of Information Act.

the Cabinet written by top bureaucrats claiming that in 1956 the Government set up an inquiry to ascertain the facts in response to public demands. This is nothing but manipulation of facts under political influence. "Sahibs" for common people, the Secretaries were servants of their political masters and they wouldn't dare to write anything in the official files that was not in conformity with the views of their boss, Prime Minister Nehru.

The bitter truth is, like in the Shastri case, the Government was totally opposed to having any public inquiry in the Netaji matter. On one hand, the officials files contain Nehru's statements that 'we are satisfied that the reports of Shri Subhas Bose's death are correct. Nothing more can be done' ; and on the other we know that Nehru was informed by a former Bose aide turned Nehru supporter, after his secret inquiry, that Japan had entrusted General Shidei to help Bose reach Russia-held territory. Foreign Secretary of that time, Subimal Dutt, scanned the records sent by this former Bose aide and spotted a hitherto unknown statement of Habibur Rahman with "significant reference to Bose's intention to get out of the plane at Dairen" in Manchuria. There was also a mention of "the intention of the Japanese authorities to let him cross over to the Russian-held territory". And yet, Nehru kept on saying publicly and on record in official files that he was convinced that Bose had died in the reported air crash and there was "absolutely no justification for appointing a commission to make further enquiries". No one uttered a word about the possibility, clearly mentioned in so many secret records, that Bose could be in Soviet Russia after his reported death—and therefore it made sense in taking up this issue with the Soviets.[5]

What eventually changed Nehru's mind—not recorded by government servants in the *sarkari* files released by the Modi government—was a threat dangled by civil society members in Calcutta that they would set up a public-funded, private enquiry to be headed by international jurist Radhabinod Pal, who was very much respected in Japan because of his pro-Japan verdict at the International Military Tribunal for the Far East. All of a sudden in 1956, Nehru formed a committee under the lead of INA hero Shah Nawaz Khan. Since they amplify the views of political masters, the official files also do not tell us that Shah Nawaz was in Netaji's INA once, but in 1956 he was

5 There have been claims that the matter was actually taken up with the Soviets in total secrecy. Rai Singh Yadav, a former senior MEA officer told me as he did to *Hindustan Times*, that as per his information Sarvepalli Radhakrishnan, then India's Ambassador in Moscow, was 'allowed to see Bose on the condition that he would not try to speak with him'.

a loyal Congress MP and a staunch Nehru supporter. In the course of his inquiry, he was made a minister. It was openly alleged thereafter that Shah Nawaz was rewarded for a "command performance". *Kya bhaijaan, deputy ministership ke liye aapne Netaji ko maar diya*! (Brother, you killed Netaji for a deputy ministership!), a niece of Netaji taunted him once.

The Shah Nawaz Committee also had for members a government officer and a representative from the Bose family—Netaji's elder brother Suresh Bose, a genial, non-political person who was thought to be non-assertive. According to a declassified note, the PM defined the task before the official inquiry panel in the following words: "The purpose of the inquiry will be to find the circumstances of the death and how far the ashes kept in a temple in Tokyo are Shri Subhas Bose's ashes". That means the air crash was a foregone conclusion for the Government, and the inquiry was to solely focus on it.

Further records show that the Japan government, which was not inclined to reopen a case from pre-1945 era that they had disowned, agreed with the Indian proposal to inquire into the Netaji matter on the condition that there would be "no departure from the main objective in view and extraneous enquiries and aside researches would not be made". The purpose of giving these minute details is to forewarn the people that in future if there's any inquiry into the Lal Bahadur Shastri episode, due care would have to be taken to prevent the establishment from putting the cart before the horse.

The Shah Nawaz Committee examined 67 witnesses in India and outside. Senior Pakistan government official Habibur Rahman's deposition before the committee in New Delhi marked his first and last appearance in India since Partition. He made a long statement in support of the air crash theory. But, after he had recorded his official version, Rahman spoke indiscreetly to Suresh Bose's right hand man Sunil Krishna Gupta: 'Let them declare that Netaji is dead. It will be our double gain when he returns!'

When the committee members met on 10 July 1956 in New Delhi, Suresh Bose enumerated a number of discrepancies and contradictions he had detected in the air crash narrative and Bose's death in Taiwan. Five days later he formally rested his case, saying he was veering towards the conclusion that there had been no plane crash at all. Shah Nawaz told Suresh Bose that in that case he would have to write a separate dissenting report. The last meeting Suresh Bose had with Shah Nawaz as a member of the Netaji Inquiry Committee was on 16 July. Shah Nawaz frowned and asked him to vacate the committee's office. "Spoilsport" Suresh was now at the receiving end of the government officers' tantrums. As per his account, he was humiliated, compelled to leave Delhi and "not a single piece of important and relevant paper or exhibit from the record" was provided to him for writing his own report.

On 29 July, Suresh Bose received a communication from Shah Nawaz demanding he should submit his dissenting report in two days. He saw the Government's hand behind the pressure tactics. A few days later Shah Nawaz's findings were leaked out to a Calcutta newspaper. Suresh immediately sent a letter to Shah Nawaz with a copy to the Prime Minister. The PM's 13 August reply brought him little comfort. Nehru theorised that the leak "was some kind of an intelligent guess by some reporter or some clerk in our office here". Angered, Suresh Bose wrote back: "When the chairman curtly turned down my request for relevant papers, I suspected that without inspiration from higher ups, he would not have had the audacity to decline the legitimate request of his colleague. My opinion has now been confirmed".

Nehru did not respond to this scathing attack accusing his government of trying to muffle Suresh's views. After some days, in a backchannel manoeuvre, Bengal Chief Minister Dr BC Roy, an old rival of Subhas Bose, called a nephew of Bose and offered him financial help if he could make his uncle Suresh agree to sign the Shah Nawaz report. When it did not work, Roy made a direct offer to Suresh Bose that governorship of Bengal awaited him. This change of course cannot be proven, just as no one today can prove the allegation that Lalita Shastri was made to keep silent for the safety of her family. But there is a shameful episode related to the Shah Nawaz's inquiry which can now be proven with the aid of official records: That the Nehru Government resorted to the doctoring of records to shore up evidence in favour of the official line.

During the course of inquiry, Shah Nawaz faced demands to carry out an on-the-spot inquiry in Taipei. Since India did not have diplomatic relations with Taiwan, the British were requested to do the needful as they maintained a consul in Taiwan. The British Consul found no real proof of Bose's death. The old Japanese records said to be of Bose turned out to be of a Japanese soldier. Like the records from the US disputing the report of Netaji's death, the reports from the British too were hushed up by the Government of India.

On 3 August 1956, the Shah Nawaz report was handed over to the Prime Minister Jawaharlal Nehru. It concluded that "Bose met his death in an air crash, and that the ashes now at Renkoji temple, Tokyo, are his ashes". The Union Cabinet approved the majority report on 9 September 1956 . According to an official record, "the Cabinet also decided that the question of bringing over Netaji's ashes to India might be left for future consideration". This betrayed the Government's lack of confidence in the report of Shah Nawaz. On September 11, a reassured Prime Minister placed the report before Parliament. Newspapers the world over carried the news prominently the next day. *The Hindu* lead story was: "Death of Netaji established: Overwhelming evidence obtained". In the Rajya Sabha, the Prime Minister adroitly fended off the few discontented lawmakers. 'Mr Nehru said the Government felt that the evidence put forth in the report was adequate and no reasonable person who read it could come to any other conclusion. If a person had an unreasonable mind, it was difficult to reason with him.'

But the committee's report came to be disputed. The Government was criticised for not letting the committee visit Taipei to carry out an on-the-spot investigation. Suresh Bose left the committee, accusing the Nehru government of trying to force him to sign on the dotted lines. He charged Shah Nawaz with manipulating evidence "so that it could easily conform with the Prime Minister's statements that Bose had died in Taipei". Helped by secret records, Sunil Krishna Gupta (who hailed from a family of revolutionaries) had obtained surreptitiously, Suresh Bose went on to write his Dissentient Report. He stated that the evidence he had come across as member of the committee proved that Subhas had escaped to the USSR. He opined that as a self-respecting and a cultured nation the Japanese helped their ally by planting fake news of his death, giving him a cover to escape, and not get caught and tried as a war criminal.

As it happened, Suresh Bose's view did not get much currency and the Government view prevailed. The case was closed. But in the 1960s it again started to made headlines for a variety of reasons. Many questions were being raised in Parliament. Some of them were based on testimonies of prominent MPs who had been told during their visit to Taiwan by that country's top officials that there was no air crash in their country involving Bose. One of those who captured public imagination was Dr Satyanarayan Sinha, a former foreign ministry official and Member of Parliament. He claimed that his sources in Taiwan and Soviet Russia informed him that there was no air crash and that Netaji was lodged in a Siberian gulag as a prisoner. The Indira Gandhi government did its best to stifle the demands for a fresh enquiry by way of a commission but public pressure became too strong to ignore. Samar Guha, a former freedom fighter turned MP, became the focal of Opposition's demand to reopen the case.

Consequently, on 11 July 1970, orders were issued for the formation of a one-man commission. Nine months later, Justice GD Khosla, a former controversial Chief Justice of the Punjab High Court, took over as its chairman. Khosla was a newsmaker in his own right and an accomplished writer. He had already earned a footnote in history as the sentencing judge in the Mahatma Gandhi assassination case. In 1947, after he moved from Lahore to Shimla, Khosla was asked to head the Fact Finding Organization to investigate cataclysmic communal violence following the partition of India. He went on to record his findings in his first book. Its brilliant prose and graphic description of the darkest period of modern Indian history have made it one of the most well-read books for that period. But Khushwant Singh thought Khosla justified as 'legitimate retaliation' the Hindu-Sikh violence against the Muslims. 'I was not aware of the anger that he harboured in his person,' he wrote of the negative trait in his friend's personality in *The Telegraph* of 25 June 2011.

The proverbial fly in the ointment was a public slight Khosla had endured during his only meeting with Subhas Bose in London in the early 1920s, when both were young ICS aspirants. Khosla happened to be passing by when Bose was telling fellow Indian students of his decision to quit the service. Khosla thought there was nothing unpatriotic in Indians substituting Englishmen in the service. Bose, in Khosla's own words, gave him 'a withering look of contempt'. VN Datta, a former president of Indian History Congress, commented in *The Tribune* in 2001 that this experience 'was bound to rankle in Khosla's heart'. It did.

By the time Khosla's inquiry neared its end in 1973, it was obvious to those watching its proceedings closely that he was biased. For instance, this time too, the Government did not want the inquiry to take place in Taiwan. However, the Opposition MPs applied pressure and the Government allowed him to go to Taiwan with a secret rider not known to anyone. In July 1973, GD Khosla landed at Taipei. Waiting for Khosla were Samar Guha and Sunil Krishna Gupta. Guha beseeched Khosla to contact the Taiwanese authorities only to be informed that the Ministry of External Affairs had already instructed the judge not to. 'Why have you come over here, then? Why did you not tell us this in Delhi?' Guha shouted.

'Why have you come to Taipei after twenty-seven years?' people asked Guha and Gupta. Somehow, they obtained permission from the Taiwanese authorities to inspect the out of bounds, unused old airstrip from where the Japanese bomber had allegedly taken off and crashed. But persuading Khosla to go there proved trickier. After he reached there, Khosla acted up. He wouldn't get off his car and when he did, he began gazing at the sky, his arms crossed on his chest, a clear sign of negative body language.

Guha tried to draw his attention to the apparent mismatch between the topography of the area and the one seen in the pictures of plane debris furnished by the Japanese to prove Bose's death. The pictures showed the debris strewn near a hill, whereas according to the survivors, and a sketch confidentially provided by the Japanese foreign office to its Indian counterpart, the plane had crashed just next to the runway. The hills, as Guha and others noted, were miles away even from the new runway. Apparently the Japanese had fobbed off to the Allies pictures of debris of some other plane. Guha turned to GD Khosla. 'Look at the pictures! Look at the hills in the background! They don't match! These pictures were planted!' Khosla became blazing mad hearing this: 'What am I to do with these pictures?'

Returning home, Guha went to Indira Gandhi to complain about Khosla's conduct. Sunil Gupta quietly slipped away to somewhere in Uttar Pradesh to brief a holy man known to his few followers as "Bhagwanji". Gupta had come to be in contact with him earlier after being tipped off by Suresh Bose. While he would not appear in public, mysterious Bhagwanji—who was later called

Gumnami Baba—was keeping an eye on the commission's work, and just about anything related to Subhas Bose. Sitting behind a curtain, he told Gupta that 'Khosla's pen was Indira's pen' and this was another 'command performance' in the making.

In June 1974, Khosla submitted his report-cum-political testament against Subhas Bose. Almost simultaneously, he released a hagiographical biography of Prime Minister Indira Gandhi, and a book on Bose's fate based on his report and experiences as chairman of the commission. Incensed by depiction of Bose as a "puppet" of the Japanese in his book, Bose's admirers went after Khosla. His nephew Dwijedranath Bose filed a suit against Khosla for trying to demean Bose.

For more than a year Khosla was literally on the run. Finally, on 1 April 1978, he, a retired High Court Chief Justice, accepted his comeuppance in a magistrate's court in Calcutta. He wriggled out of this situation of his own creation by making an unqualified apology in which he was compelled to accept that Bose was 'the liberator of our Motherland.'

In the meanwhile, Khosla's report had been tabled in Parliament and cleared without much discussion as almost all the Opposition MPs were in jail—this was the Emergency era.

The interest in the Bose mystery was revived in the mid-1990s due to the activism of Dr Purabi Roy—a professor at Kolkata's Jadavpur University. After the fall of the USSR in 1991, Roy, who spoke fluent Russian, visited Russia and was given to understand by academics and former security officials that Bose was indeed in Soviet Russia after 1945. She was told that Russian security and intelligence archives held classified records regarding Subhas Bose but they could not be accessed unless Indian government made a proper request for the same. In mid-1990s Roy inspired several stories in mainstream media that had hitherto not paid much attention to the Netaji controversy. By 1997, the matter had reached the Calcutta High Court by way of a PIL. Chief Justice Prabha Shankar Mishra and Justice B Bhattacharya asked the Government (then led by United Front) to state the official position. The Government told the court that there were doubts about Netaji's death. This prompted the court to issue an order that a new commission be set up. The new Atal Bihari Vajpayee government carried out this order and in 1999 set up a commission headed by a former Supreme Court Judge MK Mukherjee, who, unlike Shah Nawaz Khan and GD Kholsa, was not connected to the Nehru-Gandhis. One of the things the upright judge did without ever publicising it was to accept only Rs 1 as honorarium for chairing the commission. We know this now thanks to the files declassified in 2016.

While he began his inquiry on the hypothesis that Bose had died in an air crash, Justice Mukherjee nevertheless felt that "treating the oral evidence of the eyewitness about Netaji's death and cremation as axiomatically true would be non sequitur and over-simplification of and a superficial approach to this complex issue". Despite official stonewalling that he described as a "spoke in the wheel of this inquiry", Justice Mukherjee made several path-breaking findings in the course of his inquiry. He rejected the air-crash story "on the basis of robust circumstantial evidence on record". The main conclusion was that story of "the air crash, Netaji's death therein and his cremation was engineered by the Japanese army authorities".

> Obviously, in cooking up the story of Netaji's death in the plane crash and giving it a modicum of truth they (the Japanese military authorities and Habibur Rahman) had no other alternative than resorting to suppression of facts, and in doing so they not only invited material contradictions in their evidence...but also left latent loopholes which have now been discovered. ...But the question whether Netaji thereafter landed in Russia or elsewhere cannot be answered for dearth of evidence.

In addition to this, the commission found out that "the death of Ichiro Okura (a Japanese soldier) owing to heart failure on 19 August 1945, and his cremation on 22 August 1945, on the basis of a permit issued on the previous day, were passed off as those of Netaji". The Renkoji remains were actually of Okura. "The very fact that the Japanese army authorities wanted to pass off the death and cremation of Ichiro Okura as those of Netaji is an eloquent proof of their ensuring Netaji's safe passage by creating a smokescreen", Justice Mukherjee wrote. The judge tried his best to get the Renkoji temple remains examined by DNA experts, but the Government of India did not cooperate with him.

As was the case with the Khosla Commission, the Government of India did not want Justice Mukherjee to visit Taiwan. Eventually he did because I, then working for *Hindustan Times*, sought and received the official view of the Taiwan government that there was no air crash involving Netaji in August 1945. I forwarded this information and contact details to the commission. Using this, the judge was able to visit Taiwan where they officially told him as much and also provided 1945 vintage Japanese records proving that neither Bose nor General Shidei were cremated in Taiwan as was claimed earlier.[6]

The commission also investigated some other theories of Bose's fate and rejected outright all except one—the strange case of Gumnami Baba. The conclusion on this angle was that in "absence of any clinching evidence" it could not be said whether or not Gumnami Baba was Bose.

In November 2005, a staffer of the Mukherjee Commission handed over the final report to an imperious looking Home Minister Shivraj Patil. The staffer said the judge himself couldn't come as he was unwell. This was not exactly true. Justice Mukherjee had no intention to "see Patil's face". Meeting Patil's predecessor LK Advani was not as fruitful as the judge had expected, but the senior BJP leader was always courteous. Patil's undignified manner,

6 In 2018 a much-publicised claim was made by London-based journalist and Bose kin Ashis Ray in his book that Netaji did die in an air crash. Unfortunately, none of those who reviewed Ray's book inforr .d the readers that Ray is a vocal Congress party supporter and hence not a reliable narrator of facts. Ray cherry picked some portions from a jumble of contradictory statements to weave a misleading narrative to suit his political leanings. The book received much publicity because Netaji's Germany-based daughter Dr Anita Pfaff supported its finding. Again, no reviewer informed the readers that Anita was barely 2 years old when her father died and that her mother and uncles and aunts and most of the cousins rejected the air crash theory. Dr Pfaff, sadly, is known to be close to the pro-Congress faction in the Bose family. She refused to support us when we (including her elderly cousins) were hitting the streets seeking declassification of files about her father—which in itself speaks volumes about her credibility in this matter.

on the other hand, was unbecoming of a man holding the Home portfolio. In their last meeting, he did not ask Justice Mukherjee to sit down as he gave him a dressing down. He lectured that the inquiry had gone on for too long, and that too much money had been spent on it.

The commission report was arbitrarily dismissed by the Manmohan Singh government thereafter. The Memorandum of Action Taken Report tabled in Parliament in May 2006 assigned no reasons for this decision of the Government.

There was a curious development in 2010. An independent filmmaker inadvertently recorded Justice Mukherjee's off-the-record comments about Bhagwanji. The judge could be heard saying that he was '100 per cent' sure that this mostly unseen holy man was Subhas Bose. He added that he was not able to prove this in his report due to non-cooperative attitude of the Government. He hinted at a forensic fraud. There were negative reports from government DNA and handwriting exerts, even as a private handwriting expert, regarded India's No 1, gave a positive report. Since then, Mukherjee has in private conversations reiterated his belief. As far as I am concerned, an honest and upright Supreme Court judge is a much more credible person than the likes of Shivraj Patil or government "servants" who write official records.

When it appeared that everything was over, in 2013, the Allahabad High Court pronounced a judgment[7] over the Bhagwanji controversy. The court asked the state government to display his belongings at a museum and formed a commission of inquiry with a host of experts to ascertain who this man was in view of the claims that he was Netaji. My efforts were lauded by the court in its order.[8] The court saw some merit in the arguments in favour of the Bhagwanji theory. Otherwise, the case would have been dismissed in no time as the proposition that Netaji could be alive and remain in hiding in India for such a long time is patently preposterous. But things are not what they always seem. In my books, *India's Biggest Cover-Up* (2012) and a somewhat more up to date but concise *What Happened to Netaji?* (2015), I have demonstrated that the Bhagwanji theory cannot be ignored. It was *India's Biggest Cover-Up* which prompted the family of Netaji to come out on the streets and demand

7 The court order was in response to a PIL filed by Netaji's niece Lalita Bose in 1986 and subsequently by Shakti Singh, in whose house the mostly unseen Bhagwanji stayed the last in Faizabad.

8 The court order reads that my journalistic enquiry 'seems to be genuine and based on relevant material' and that my books 'prima facie makes out a case for a probe' into the identity of Gumnami Baba. 'The State and Central Governments should look into it to remove doubts with regard to Gumnami Baba by holding appropriate enquiry.'

declassification of the files. It also inspired the making of the hit webseries "Bose: Dead/Alive" by Ekta Kapoor, one of the top names in Hindi film industry.

Meanwhile, for one reason or the other, the UP government couldn't make its mind about the HC order. On 13 February 2016, a delegation comprising Subhas Bose's kin and Mission Netaji members and others, most prominently activist Adheer Som and Shakti Singh (in whose house Gumnami Baba last stayed), met Chief Minister Akhilesh Singh Yadav. This resulted in the formation of a commission in June 2016 under the chairmanship of Justice Vishnu Sahai, a former acting Chief Justice of Allahabad High Court. Unfortunately, this inquiry proved an exercise in futility because the judge carried out a perfunctory inquiry, which was unlikely to yield anything. From the start, the judge showed little inclination for trying to understand the complexity of the case. To give two examples; Justice Sahai refused to summon and take evidence from Justice Mukherjee (who used to be his senior as the Chief Justice of Allahabad High Court), over his statement about Bhagwanji. Second, Justice Sahai ignored the demand made by Chandrachur Ghose and me to summon Subramanian Swamy over his claim that Bhagwanji was an IB plant and then verify those claims from the Intelligence Bureau. (Anyhow, a most comprehensive account of the so-called Gumnami Baba will shortly be released by Chandrachur Ghose and me. Our book will provide sufficient evidence to support the view that Bhagwanji/Gumnami Baba was Netaji indeed). Against all this, we have to assess the claim that there is a link between Shastriji's death and Subhas Bose. As stated before, the very idea would stand rejected if Netaji died in 1945. Now that it seems he did not, and he even might have been the so-called Gumnami Baba, we need to assess this aspect in this light.

Going by the official records that have been released, Shastri's view regarding Netaji was similar to the one taken by the Nehru government. We have seen from the declassified CIA records that upon assuming prime ministership he ran the government more or less in the same way as Nehru did. But he was deferential towards Subhas Bose—seven years his senior in age. In the Lok Sabha on 29 March 1965, a member asked Shastri about Netaji, adding that 'there is a fear in the minds of many people who still believe that Netaji is alive, that he is regarded as a war criminal by the Britishers. They want a clear declaration from the Government regarding this.' Shastri's reply to this was: 'So far as Netaji Subhas Chandra Bose is concerned, of course, there is absolutely no doubt in the mind of anyone in this country that he would be welcome here as one of our greatest heroes.' Some people interpret it as an indication that he was open to the idea that Netaji could be alive.

Then there were others who did not get that impression as Shastri ignored or did not approve of demands to reopen the Subhas Bose disappearance case. On 7 August 1964, Amiya Nath Bose, Netaji's nephew, sent him copies of his correspondence with Nehru just before he passed away. Amiya drew Shastri's attention to the Prime Minister's remark that something should be done to "finalise the question of Netaji's death". Amiya asked Shastri to take appropriate steps. On 12 August Shastri wrote back that he would look into the matter.

'Unfortunately Shri Shastri did not take any further steps in this matter,' Amiya noted when he heard nothing from the PM. But at the official level, Shastri had actually taken up the matter with Bengal Chief Minister Prafulla Chandra Sen through a Top Secret letter dated 2 September 1964. Forwarding copy of the letter Nehru had written to Amiya, the Prime Minister commented: "I am afraid Shri Bose's conclusion that Panditji had agreed to his suggestion for a judicial inquiry is not borne by this letter". He added: "I really do not know what further can be done about this matter". Sen advised Shastri in his reply that "in view of the categorical reply[9] of Panditji to Shri Suresh Bose in August 1962, I do not think there is anything further that can be done".

Amiya again wrote to Shastri on 7 May 1965, drawing his attention to newspaper stories reporting sensational claims of Dr Satyanarayan Sinha. Amiya sent two more reminders but he was not "favoured with any reply". Not everything is written down, we must bear in mind, when it comes to sensitive matters. Probably Shastri was waiting for an opportune time; perhaps he was making up his mind. Most of the communication within governments is verbal of which no record is made. In any case, there is a record from August 1965 showing that the Indian embassy did informally take up with the Soviet Foreign Office the claim of Sinha that Netaji was imprisoned in their country. Hearing this, an official of the South Asia Division said that he had already seen this report in the Indian newspapers. "He stated that he could only

9 Irked by Nehru's 7 May 1962 statement in the Lok Sabha that 'the basic conclusions reached by the committee have never been seriously questioned', Suresh Bose dared Nehru to furnish 'proof' of his brother's death. Prime Minister Nehru in his response stated that the proof was circumstantial, not 'precise and direct'. 'In addition to this, the lapse of time now and the extreme probability of his being alive secretly somewhere when he would be welcomed in India with great joy and affection, adds to that circumstantial evidence'.

comment in a personal capacity. He said that there was no basis whatsoever in the story and added that he could not escape the feeling that the story was a 'mischievous invention'."

Now that we have the statement of Chandra Kumar Bose that Shastri did speak with his father Amiya Nath Bose before leaving for Tashkent and said that he would 'search evidence of Netaji's presence in Russia' during his visit, we need to explore this matter differently. A different picture emerges when we consider Shastriji's expressions concerning Netaji in his private talks with people who were close to him and had no reasons or motive to tell lies. First is a brief but astoundingly suggestive account that Sanjay Nath Singh, Shastri's grandson, gave me. He said that his mother Suman asked her father whether Netaji was still alive or something to that effect. Shastri was then Prime Minister. He looked at his daughter over the edge of his spectacles, smiled and scratched his head, looking amused. 'That was his way of telling his daughter that he was not very sure, or that there was something he couldn't tell her,' Singh explained to me. Shastriji could have easily repeated the official view that Bose died a long time ago.

For good measure, the second instance of Shastri speaking about Netaji was brought on record. This was before the Khosla Commission in 1972. Former Delhi

Congress chief and Shastri's confidant Jagdish Kodesia made a series of startling claims in his 'on oath' deposition. He recalled that after Nehru's last rites were performed, Shastri, for some strange reasons, was thinking about Netaji, officially dead way back in 1945.

> When we were returning after the cremation of Panditji, Shastriji said after seeing the huge crowds: 'Could you imagine that this type of crowd would collect spontaneously if it were declared that Netaji is coming to Delhi on such and such date?' I said: 'I do not think there will be a single man, woman or child sitting in the house, they will all come to greet him.' He smiled at me, though the occasion was sad.[10]

Kodesia even testified that during the 1962 war he heard at Shastri's house that "information during Chinese aggression did come that Netaji was living". In fact, there is a formerly Top Secret record in which the then Director, Intelligence Bureau is referring to "propaganda"

---

10 Kodesia's statement is part of the record of proceedings of Khosla Commission. Running into thousands of pages, it was declassified in 2010 following the long-drawn efforts of Chandrachur Ghose and sent to the National Archives in Delhi.

that Netaji would return was "started when the Chinese invaded our country". Several times during his deposition, Kodesia linked the Bose mystery to the controversy surrounding Prime Minister Lal Bahadur Shastri's sudden death. He claimed Shastri was thinking of reopening the Netaji "death" case. 'If he would have lived any longer, he would have seen to that,' he said, in what was a spine-chilling comment.

If Subhas Chandra Bose had really met his end in the era of Joseph Stalin (1922–1953), as Subramanian Swamy claims, then there was no question of Shastri thinking about his return in 1962. These statements, however, gel with the narrative emerging from the claims of Bhagwanji. In brief, he claimed that in order to continue his fight for India, he sought help from the Russians towards the end of the war. He claimed that he made a secret trip to Moscow in December. There is a declassified intelligence report from 1946 which refers to such a secret visit of Netaji to Soviet Union. Bhagwanji claimed there was no air crash; he escaped to Russia. He said he was well taken care of by them, and remained in hiding in Siberia for some years.

This incredible narrative further holds that in time, Bhagwanji—he preferred the term "Dead Man" for himself—became involved in Soviet covert operations to undermine the American hegemony in South East Asia and elsewhere with the larger aim to ensure that India was not caught in bloody proxy wars between the free and communist worlds. Because of his covert activities and unpublicised role in international events, and not due to the "war criminal" tag of the second world war, Bhagwanji thought he was regarded as "Enemy No 1" by the world powers. In his estimate, if he emerged, people of India would have suffered as there would have been economic sanctions and other instances of arm-twisting to ensure his capture, which would have been opposed tooth-and-nail by his supporters in India. So, when asked why he was not emerging, he would say it was 'not in India's interest.'

As would be detailed in our forthcoming book, Bhagwanji said he maintained contacts with the Russians throughout, and he would often travel secretly to Russia even after he surreptitiously returned to India in mid-1950s. He claimed that the top Russian leadership were beholden to him for the "help" he had provided on strategic and diplomatic fronts. The available accounts show that Bhagwanji's presence in India was known to many top leaders. It is my estimate that after Nehru was gone the Government knew about him, and that he was unable to emerge.

Bhagwanji hinted that Shastri, towards whom he was more or less kindly disposed, was aware of his existence.

But, whether they ever came face to face or even had a direct contact is not clear. Bhagwanji made a series of mindboggling claims, including those about the India-Pakistan war of 1965 and the subsequent Tashkent conference. He was critical of Indian leaders in general and claimed that he provided military inputs during the war but rued that they were not used to the hilt to run down Pakistan completely. He did not approve of the idea of having a summit in Tashkent, feeling that it was not in India's interests, and that Russians were merely interested in furthering their diplomatic clout at the expense of India's vital interests. He had some of his ideas conveyed through some unspecified channels to Shastri. He thought that Shastri responded to these ideas of his by way of some of his public statements at that time. He wondered whether Shastri's decision to visit Calcutta and unveil the first proper statue[11] of Netaji in India had something to do with his all this.

Bhagwanji wanted Shastri to invite the Russians to

11 Joined by his wife, Shastriji visited Calcutta on 24 December 1965, which was somewhat strange because it made more sense for him to undertake this visit a month later on January 23, Subhas Bose's birth anniversary. Anyhow, it was during this visit that Shastri met Bose's nephew Amiya and, as Chandra Bose says, told him that he'd do something about the Netaji issue when he was in Soviet Russia.

India, rather than going there himself. In his words, Shastri 'lost his mind' when he took the decision to go there. He said this remorsefully because he was grief-stricken when he heard that Lal Bahadur—as he would call him—had suddenly died. Like so many others, he suspected that the death was not natural but what he felt beyond that or if he had anyone in mind for a suspect, I am not aware. Since Russia continued to figure in his talks and letters, one can safely say he did not blame the Soviets at least.

Assuming that Bhagwanji was indeed Netaji, was he really in Tashkent at the time the accord was signed? Bhagwanji did talk about what happened in closed door meetings in Tashkent, but he did not suggest that it was a first-hand account. In fact, one of his closest followers who is still living, told me in no uncertain terms that Bhagwanji was in India at that time and he was bed-ridden due to high fever. In none of his numerous letters and conversations, in which he made one startling claim after another, Bhagwanji ever said he was in Tashkent at that time. So what then is the worth of the reports that "Netaji" was seen during the signing of the Tashkent accord?

To quote *The Times of India* on 12 December 2015, "in the first ever visual evidence of Subhas Bose two decades after he was declared dead in an alleged plane crash, Netaji researchers have produced a forensic face-mapping report by a British expert that has found strong resemblance between Bose and a man photographed with former PM Lal Bahadur Shastri during the Indo-Pak peace talks in Tashkent in 1966". The researchers called a press meet in Kolkata to publicise the report sent to them from abroad. "The forensic face mapping was commissioned by former Mission Netaji member and Dutch national of Indian origin Siddharth Satbhai", the TOI report said.

Facial mapping involves comparing two sets of images (pictures as well as videos) of individuals by experts to determine whether or not they are of the same person. A lot depends on the quality of the imagery available in order to reach a firm conclusion. In some countries, facial mapping reports are admitted in courts as corroborative evidence.

The most impressive aspect of the sensational claim of spotting Netaji in Tashkent relates to the credentials of the expert who carried out this test. A veteran of British army's Royal Corps of Signals, Neil Miller is an experienced facial mapping, CCTV and height analysis expert. He has presented expert opinion in cases at UK high courts. In his report, he gave the opinion "that serious consideration must be given to the contention that the Tashkent Man and Subhas Chandra Bose share very similar facial features and could potentially be one and the same person".

Imagery, both still and moving that has been supplied to me, in regard to the historical facial features of Subhas Chandra Bose and the individual identified as the Tashkent Man, lends support leaning towards strong support to the contention that they are one and the same person.

At the same time, Miller has made some qualifications to his conclusion. He has made it clear that his report is "not suitable for Court and therefore should not be used as such". In other words, it cannot be treated as evidence.[12]

He also states that should additional imagery or information of the Tashkent Man or Subhas Chandra Bose be provided, "the result of my analysis might change".

As someone who supports the Bhagwanji angle of the Netaji disappearance mystery I should have latched on to this revelation and used it to bolster my case, but I did not. That's because I see no facial resemblance between Subhas Chandra Bose and the so-called Tashkent man, who doesn't appear to be 69 years old as Netaji would have been in 1966. Netaji had taken after his mother

12 Handwriting expert's opinion in the Bhagwanji/Gumnami Baba matter was treated as evidence as the expert deposed before the Justice Mukherjee Commission and was cross-examined on oath by the judge and others.

and many of his living family members have partially Mongoloid facial features similar to his. In that sense, I can visualise how Netaji was in real life. The Tashkent man does not, to my eyes, appear anything like that. Facial mapping reports do not prove anything in isolation; they need to corroborate something. To best of my knowledge, Bhagwanji was not in Tashkent at that time; he was in UP and ailing. Plus, he was opposed to the Tashkent talks and did not want Shastri to join them.

I am also not clear about the bona fides of Siddharth Satbhai, the PIO who supplied the pictures, etc. to Neil Miller and obtained the report. I have serious reservations about the credentials of the leading members of the "Siddharth Satbhai Support Team" who released the report in Calcutta Press Club in December 2015. The leader of this team of so-called "Netaji researchers" was Rajyashree Chaudhuri, a Hindu Mahasabha leader and distant relative of Subhas Bose. Rajyashree is known for making preposterous claims about Subhas Bose. Prior to the Tashkent Man claim, Chaudhuri captured some sort of media attention in 2015 alleging that Netaji had been tortured to death in Soviet Russia at the behest of Pandit Nehru. After some time, she changed her stand to say that Bhagwanji was Netaji, adding that he was alive long after his death in 1985.

The main researcher associated with the "Siddharth Satbhai Support Team" was Dr Jayanta Choudhury, editor of a Bengali paper. Choudhury reveres a holy man called Balak Brahmachari, who set up a cult group whose members are vociferous in claiming publicly that Netaji is still alive without offering any reasoning or proof. On social media and elsewhere, members of this cult group made the most of the "Netaji in Tashkent" theory. In many places in Bengal, these people are taken to be Subhas Bose's followers, whereas they are essentially the followers of Balak Brahmachari—who just happened to know about the existence of Bhagwanji.

In 1993, when Brahmachari passed away, the followers claimed that he had merely entered into a *nirvikalp samadhi* and would come back to life. This led to much drama in those days and was widely reported in media, both in India and abroad. After a 55-day stand-off, Brahmachari's mortal remains were seized by the police and cremated. Today, while some of his followers let lose a stream of invective against anyone who doesn't agree with their rants that Subhas Chandra Bose is still alive, others hold in highest esteem former President Pranab Mukherjee, who they claimed took *diksha* from Balak Brahmachari. There are pictures showing Mukherjee touching the feet of Brahmachari.

Former President of India, Pranab Mukherjee, is universally respected. But in the context of the Netaji death matter, he has a different image. His support for the air crash theory of Subhas Bose's death hasn't gone down well with many. In 1995, he approached Netaji's wife Emilie Schenkl to sign a document confirming his death so that his presumptive ashes could be brought to India. Emilie refused as she believed Bose was in Russia after his reported death. Mukherjee defended the arbitrary and undemocratic rejection of the report of Justice MK Mukherjee Commission of Inquiry in 2006. As stated earlier, the Netaji mystery is a complex, multi-layered matter with much intrigue.

As for Siddharth Satbhai, in 2015 he dropped "Netaji" from nowhere right into the middle of a major diplomatic conference 20 years after his reported death. He wouldn't say anything about what Netaji was doing in Tashkent, for what reasons and where had he been for all those years. This silence was for a reason. Siddharth came into contact with me years ago. It was from me he got the idea that Bose lived in the guise of a holy man in several parts of UP. He would occasionally go out of India, mostly with the help of Russians.

It was at my instance that Siddharth started locating pictures of a bearded man spotted in the course of a session of Paris peace talks concerning the Vietnam war. Bhagwanji had claimed that he was present in one of these talks, and also gave the reasons why he was there. Siddharth was able to locate a picture where a person resembling Netaji could be seen. He was good enough to buy its rights and transferred the same to me for use in my book *India's Biggest Cover-Up*.[13] The idea of facial mapping was also jointly developed by us over this picture.

What happened subsequently is not very clear to me. Did something change Siddharth or was he up to mischief from the very start? In the course of his search for Paris peace talks pictures for me, Siddharth uncovered much more than what he has made public. He told me and my "Mission Netaji" friends that he met a former French intelligence officer who confirmed to him that the bearded man spotted during the Paris peace talks in 1969 was indeed Subhas Bose. This retired intelligence officer was actually present at the venue and he said that the CIA had sought the French authorities' help in tracking the bearded man by taking measures such as lifting his fingerprints, etc.

I cannot confirm whether Siddharth was telling the

13 I did not claim that this bearded man was Bhagwanji or Netaji. I was led to it because of Bhagwanji's sayings. So I explored this matter just as I've delved into several theories about the Shastriji matter in this volume.

truth or making it all up. In a subsequent meeting, this French officer gave Siddharth a report which contained Bose's name clearly in the context of Paris peace talks. He also provided close-up pictures, including coloured ones, of the bearded man, seeing which Siddharth was convinced that the man was Netaji. Siddharth went on to tell me that according to the French officer (and report), Bose was on the radar of Western intelligence agencies as reports and sightings about him from different parts of the world flummoxed them. This intelligence officer was astonished when Siddharth gave him a copy of my book and explained that Bhagwanji was based in India.

Being in "possession" of the report and Paris man pictures, Siddharth began telling us that he had obtained clinching evidence to support the view that Bose was alive after 1945. Quite naturally, we wanted him to go public with the pictures and intelligence report—but he started saying that he feared for his personal safety and the safety of his family. In the course of our talks, he told me that he feared Russian intelligence agency SVR RF—one of the two successors of the old KGB—in particular. That they were very ruthless and would not like the disclosures he was in a position to make. He told me about the poisoning of a former KGB officer (Alexander Litvinenko) in the United Kingdom. My friends and I made several attempts to convince Siddharth to go public with all that he had. He said he could not due to security reasons. We then asked him to hand over the material to us so that we could release it, but he was not willing.

Eventually, Siddharth dropped the idea of releasing explosive information he said he had about the bearded man. I imagine he calculated that doing so would only support the line I had taken in my book. Since he evidently wanted the limelight only on himself, Siddharth came up with the Tashkent man theory, which was novel and entirely his creation. Eventually Siddharth was able to go public with his theory—but with no background details.

In December 2016, Siddharth muddied the waters further by releasing a picture of his with Sharmistha Mukherjee, President Pranab Mukherjee's daughter and Congress party spokesperson. She was one of the spokespersons fielded by the party to speak in favour of the air crash theory of Netaji's death when the matter came to be discussed on TV channels in 2015 and subsequently. I respect Ms Mukherjee as a person, but after years of research, I do not trust the Congress party and those associated with it over matters relating to Netaji Subhas Chandra Bose.

ELEVEN

Towards a closure

AS IF BY a divine design, fifty-two years after the tragedy in Tashkent, the best ever opportunity to seek a final closure to one of India's most enduring controversies is heading our way. With little luck, the scene that is going to unfold might just replicate what happened in America in 1991. That year, filmmaker Oliver Stone turned conspiracy theories surrounding the assassination of John F Kennedy in 1963 into a riveting film—*JFK*. This in turn channelised the pent-up feelings of Americans, their long-standing desire to know the truth about who all were responsible for the ghastly shooting in Dallas. The film opened with an emotive quote of Ella Wheeler Wilcox: "To sin by silence, when we should protest, makes cowards out of men". Despite critics reviling it in numerous reviews, *JFK* became a runaway hit. Roger Ebert, the first film critic to win the Pulitzer Prize for Criticism, was one of those who viewed the movie favourably. In his view, its achievement lay in the fact that it marshalled "the anger which ever since 1963 has been gnawing away on some dark shelf of the national psyche".

In Vivek Agnihotri's upcoming film *The Tashkent Files* there is similar potential. Unusual for a Bollywood personality, Agnihotri is a noted thinker and commentator too—a child of freedom fighter parents. The *Tashkent Files* began trending on social media from the day the first word about it was put out. Its impressive star cast, includes Naseeruddin Shah, Mithun Chakraborty and Shweta Basu Prasad. A movie is the most potent way of drawing the public to an issue. And so, with the release of *The Tashkent Files*, the Shastri death issue should come under the spotlight like never before.

A comparatively happy closure to this sad saga would have been attained long ago had the Government set up a public inquiry under the supervision of the Supreme Court. The least the Government could have done was to make public all records concerning the tragedy in Tashkent and then given MPs and the media full access to question the eyewitnesses and other officials, like our Ambassador in Moscow, who witnessed the tragedy unfolding.

But nothing of this sort ever happened because the

Government was firm in its resolve to keep a lid on the controversy. Though there were repeated demands, a proper inquiry was ruled out on the false pretext that there was nothing to suspect. To contain public outrage, there was a partial disclosure, but key eyewitnesses such as Dr Chugh were kept in complete isolation. A blow by blow account by the doctor and other eyewitnesses to even a Parliamentary committee would have nipped the controversy in the bud. In the course of a discussion in Parliament, the Government said it would make Dr Chugh available to the lawmakers for questioning, but it was not done. I see merit in the charge that the eyewitnesses were under some sort of duress because in the course of my research I have not come across even a single media report based on accounts provided by them. It made sense for leading publications, from *Dharmyug* to *Hindustan Times*, to carry interviews with Dr Chugh, Ram Nath and others. When Subhas Chandra Bose was reported dead in 1945 so many of those who had (or claimed to have) direct information about his last days freely aired their views in newspapers, even though India was not a free country and the second world war had just ended.

Hence, it is clear that the Government mishandled the Shastri death matter in 1966 and beyond. What could have been the reason? One way of looking at it is that probably the Government fumbled because no one knew how to handle a tragedy of such proportions. Gulzarilal Nanda was but a caretaker Prime Minister. Numbed by the totally unexpected turn of events and weighed down by apprehensions of complicating relations with a friendly superpower soon after a war with a neighbour, those in charge did not do what should have been done. Shastriji was sadly gone and there was nothing to be achieved by splitting hairs over a case of natural death. Life is all about moving forward.

The other explanation is that something did go wrong in Tashkent. Of all the allegations of foul play, the accusations against the Americans were complete nonsense; those against Russians misplaced. My personal views notwithstanding, the Netaji link to this case won't come in the reckoning till it is proven that the freedom fighter was very much alive after his reported death in 1945. All we are left with are grave questions about the acts of omission and commission on the part of our Government, especially Ambassador (later Foreign Secretary) TN Kaul. Why did the Government not inquire into the Shastri fake letter case? Was it for fear that it would bring the death controversy into the spotlight? Why were the people of India given a false narrative that there was nothing amiss even though the Russians suspected poisoning the moment Shastri died? Why did the Government insist that there was nothing to doubt about the credentials of Mohammed Jan even though he had been picked for interrogation by the KGB? Why was the nation misled about the position of the telephone in Shastri's suite? Why did the Government ignore the condition in which Shastri's body arrived in India? Why was sandal paste smeared on Shastri's face when his family members pointed out that it was defaced? Why didn't Health Minister Sushila Nayyar, an eminent doctor and Gandhiji's close aide, take any action? Dahyabhai Patel surely had a point when he observed that there was something sinister here 'for not even the most hidebound bureaucrat would have forbidden his nearest and dearest to approach Shastri's body' unless he knew for sure that there was something to be concealed.

The charge of a cover-up is not only on the Indira Gandhi government but also on subsequent governments. No effort seems to have been made by anyone thereafter. There was a controversy about Dr Ram Manohar Lohia's death in October 1967, following an operation at Delhi's Wellington Hospital (now named after Lohia). In response to Opposition charges and demands for an inquiry, the Indira Gandhi-led government stated that a review of the treatment record by senior medical officers revealed no negligence of any sort. In 1977, when Janata Party took over, a committee inquired into the matter and found complacency in both pre-operative and post-operative stages. Since no post-mortem was performed, the exact cause of death could not be pinpointed and therefore it was impossible to fix the blame on any one individual. On the Netaji issue, the same government made some progress by accepting that the findings of inquiries set up by previous Congress-led governments were not conclusive. So why didn't the Morarji Desai government look into the Shastri case as was rumoured earlier that a committee under Raj Narain would be set up? Was it due to Desai's personal belief? Did it have anything to with his past rivalry with Shastri? One can only speculate. According to Kuldip Nayar, Desai formed an opinion that there was no foul play after speaking with Dr Chugh[1] and CP Srivastava.

A golden chance was missed from late 80s onwards when Soviet Russia was tottering and all sorts of KGB records were emerging from secret vaults. Universities in the West made the best of the situation and accessed so many of them. Even governments tried. Boris Yeltsin,

1 By the time Desai took over as PM, Dr Chug was dead. So he must have consulted him during the period Indira Gandhi was Prime Minister.

the new Russian leader, was open to requests. There was a conspiracy theory linking the Soviets to Kennedy's assassination. Yeltsin put an end to it in 1999, when he personally handed over to US President Bill Clinton about 80 documents related to the assassination originating from the Russian intelligence archives.

The disclosure in the *Soviet Land* in 1991 that Shastri's room in the dacha was bugged and that the intelligence officials heard (and most likely recorded) whatever happened in the Indian leader's last moments should have been immediately followed up by the Ministry of External Affairs with the Russian Foreign Ministry. In fact, Sunil Shastri wrote to then Prime Minister Chandrashekhar about it but received a one line answer. I consider this lapse inexcusable because we have on record an instance when something about Netaji on the basis of KGB records was going to be published in Russia in the 1990s and our Government tried to prevent it from happening after it got wind of it. Under pressure from Netaji's followers, VP Singh's government first raised the matter of Netaji with Russia, albeit in an inadequate manner. The Narasimha Rao government was compelled as well and it too made a half-hearted effort. But there were no such efforts over the Shastriji matter. The Ministry of External Affairs in its first RTI response to me said that it had no information concerning the death of a Prime Minister of India dying abroad. When in my next RTI application I underlined that it was just not possible, they brazenly stated the information could not be given for fear of spoiling foreign relations.

This is all history now. So what is it that can be done at this point in time when just about everyone having any direct knowledge of what happened in Tashkent is dead? As I see it, the onus is on us to do what those before us could not. The future generations would not have the drive to act, as the emotional connect to Shastri would have faded away with the passage of time. At the same time, posterity will hold us responsible for neglecting such a poignant matter. The Government may like it or not, but *The Tashkent files* and this book are going to have a lasting impact on the minds of countless Indians and people of Indian origin across the world.

In order to resolve the controversy surrounding the death of Lal Bahadur Shastri, we would need to handle it with the same seriousness usually given to cases that are politically volatile, sensational and even sleazy. High ideals of truth and justice are invoked, and heaven and hell are moved to ascertain facts in such instances. Recall the Bhanwari Devi murder case of 2012. This was about a woman who had disappeared after her extra-marital affair with a local minister became public knowledge. An inquiry was carried out in right earnest. The CBI sleuths actually went all over Rajasthan with a fine tooth-comb and managed to dig out from a remote village, pieces of bones thought to be hers. These bones were then sent all the way to the United States, so that the Federal Bureau of Investigation could find out if these indeed were of the missing woman. The FBI sent a positive reply and this is how the case was cracked. This was such an incredible thing happening in a country where the Government refused to get a DNA test done on the so-called remains of Netaji, and many historians feel that there is no need to probe his death because it would be a waste of time and money as he won't return to us.

Though it happened so many decades ago, the Shastriji death controversy deserves to be pursued with the same vigour as seen in cases involving people who were nowhere close to Shastri in stature. On 12 January 2018, an unprecedented national crisis erupted from the most unlikely quarters. As reported in news website *The Wire*, "Four justices of the Supreme Court—the seniormost justices after the Chief Justice of India—decided to hold a press conference to talk about the issues plaguing the apex court, triggered by issues surrounding a case on the death of special CBI Judge BH Loya and the roster of justices at the Supreme Court".[2] The shock waves, as we all know, reverberated across the country soon after the extraordinary press meet.

The Congress party lost no time in issuing a statement which, among other things, underlined the judges' referring to a PIL concerning Loya's death, "which the family of the Judge believes was under suspicious circumstances". The statement further said: "In the PIL concerning the death of Judge Loya, we believe that the matter must be entrusted to the seniormost judges of the Supreme Court who should ensure that under their supervision there is a thorough and impartial investigation of the case by an independent SIT." Articulating the ruling party's stand, Sambit Patra, BJP spokesperson said they were surprised that the Congress was 'trying to gain political mileage' over an 'internal matter' of the apex court. 'No politics should be played,' said the BJP spokesperson.

In a way, the "controversy" surrounding the death of Judge Loya was similar to Shastriji's. Brijgopal Harkishan Loya was the judge presiding over a case involving the extra-judicial killing of gangster Sohrabuddin Sheikh in

---

2 **Loya Case the Tipping Point, Four SC Judges Say Democracy Is in Danger**. Accessed from: https://thewire.in/law/sc-justices-hold-historic-press-conference-triggered-judge-loya-case.

2005. The killing was alleged to have been carried out by senior police officers at the behest of Gujarat's Home Minister Amit Shah, now president of the BJP. Loya was in 2014 appointed to the special CBI court in Mumbai hearing the Sohrabuddin matter. The Supreme Court had in 2012 moved the trial to the city in view of apprehensions expressed by some people that Shah might try to influence witnesses in his home state. In October 2014, Loya set the date of the judgment day as 15 December. However, on 1 December, in Nagpur, 48-years-old Loya suddenly passed away following a cardiac arrest he suffered after attending the marriage ceremony of a colleague's daughter. The death was witnessed by his colleagues, who were judges themselves. After Loya's death, his successor judge in the CBI court dismissed all charges against Shah in the Sohrabuddin Sheikh case. This was on 30 December 2014.

Three years later, a series of articles appeared in news magazine *The Caravan* raising doubts about Loya's death. This is where the similarity between the Shastriji and Judge Loya cases end. The Congress party latched on to the issue from the word go. On 31 January 2018, former Law Minister and noted lawyer, Kapil Sibal, flanked by former Minister of External Affairs and lawyer, Salman Khurshid, and party spokesperson, Randeep Singh Surjewala, told media persons that if there was no proper probe into the matter, the party will go to 'each village of the country.' Alleging that 'democracy is in danger', Sibal introduced a lawyer from Nagpur, who he claimed was privy to "pressure" Loya was under due to the high-profile case he was handling. The documents relating to Loya's post-mortem were also "manipulated", Sibal claimed. 'We can't talk about how he (Loya) died... but the circumstances are telling some story,' he said. 'Our demand is that this matter must be referred to an independent SIT where there is no CBI officer, where there is no NIA officer. This independent SIT must be chosen, if this investigation is to go on.'[3] According to a report in *The Wire*, the party also "raised questions about what it said were the unexplained deaths of lawyer activist Shrikant Khandalkar and retired judge Prakash Thombre". Congress leaders alleged that "Loya had confided in Khandalkar and Thombre about the pressure he was facing to exonerate the accused in the Sohrabuddin murder case".[4]

This was followed by the press conference of the Supreme Court judges against the Chief Justice of India

3 **Judge Loya death case: Congress raises more questions**, *Financial Express*, 31 January 2018.

4 **Congress for Probe Into Loya's Death, Sees Foul Play in Death of Two Associates**. Accessed from: https://thewire.in/law/congress-will-collaborate-if-sc-sets-up-sit-to-probe-loyas-death-kapil-sibal.

and, on 19 April, an order by the Supreme Court on a PIL seeking an inquiry into the Loya death matter. This had been filed by Congress leader Tehseen Poonawalla. On 12 January, Poonawalla had alleged that he was pressurised by a senior advocate to withdraw his petition. Refusing to divulge the name of this advocate, he said he had 'full faith in the judiciary. I have nothing to do with the politics surrounding the case.'[5]

Chief Justice Dipak Misra and Justices AM Khanwilkar and DY Chandrachud dismissed Poonawalla's petition, finding no ground "to hold that there was a reasonable suspicion about the cause or circumstances of death which would merit a further inquiry". Rather than bowing to the SC verdict, the Congress questioned it, which, to my understanding, was another attempt to bring the apex court into disrepute. The party dubbed the verdict "a sad day in India's history". ANI quoted Congress spokesperson RS Surjewala as saying during a press conference that the verdict had 'left many questions unanswered. There were discrepancies in the post-mortem report, even in recording the name of the victim properly.' Senior leader and lawyer

5 **I was pressured to withdraw Loya plea in SC: Congress leader Tehseen Poonawalla**. Accessed from: https://timesofindia.indiatimes.com/india/i-was-pressured-to-withdraw-loya-plea-in-sc-congress-leader-tehseen-poonawalla/articleshow/62479621.cms.

Abhishek Manu Singhvi tweeted that 'dispassionate analysis of Loya judgement must await its full reasoning. But unless logical reasons found in it, it will raise more questions and leave many unanswered'.

Never mind what the Congress leaders said, a reading of the judgment reveals that the Supreme Court explored every charge that was levelled. At the very beginning, the verdict reproduces *The Caravan* reports on the basis of which the petition was filed by Poonawalla for what he claimed was "for the welfare and benefit of the society as a whole...with no ulterior or mala fide motive". There were other petitioners as well but they all relied on the same magazine reports, as well as reports published in *The Indian Express*, *Quint*, *The Wire* and *Scroll*. Some of these publications are said to be biased in favour of the Congress party.

Just to give a small illustration, the following was claimed in *The Caravan* articles:

- Loya was taken to hospital in an auto rickshaw.
- Ishwar Baheti, an RSS worker, informed Loya's father that he would arrange for the body to reach Gategaon. Nobody knows why, how and when he came to know about the death of Brij Loya.
- To the family's shock, none of Loya's colleagues had

accompanied his body on the journey from Nagpur. The only person accompanying the body was the ambulance driver.

- Post-mortem and histo-pathology reports were sent to a forensic expert, Dr RK Sharma, formerly attached to AIIMS. Dr Sharma ruled out the possibility of the death being due to a heart attack. Documents indicate signs of trauma to the brain. Hence, it was urged that poisoning cannot be ruled out.
- Loya's body carried bloodstains on the neck at the back of the shirt.

And these are the responses the court found to be truthful:

- Judge Loya was taken to hospital in the car of a fellow judge.
- Loya's father confirmed that Ishwar Govindlal Baheti was his son's childhood friend. Baheti was associated with the Congress party. He came to know about Loya's health from his doctor brother. *The Caravan* apparently confused him with one Ishwar Prasad Bajranglal Baheti, who used to be active in the RSS long ago (which, in my view, might have inspired the reporter to cook up a conspiracy theory with a view to drag the RSS into the case).
- Loya's body was sent to village Gategaon in Latur in an ambulance. Two judicial magistrates from Nagpur

were deputed by Principal District Judge, Nagpur, to accompany the body.

- Dr RK Sharma clarified he was grossly misquoted by *The Caravan*. 'The conclusions drawn are imaginary.'
- When clothes are put back on the body after autopsy by the mortuary attendants, the precision and neatness of clothing cannot be compared to the way a living person may dress. After autopsy examination is over, the incisions over neck, chest, abdomen and head on the dead body are sutured after putting the dissected organs back into the cavities. In spite of every precaution being taken to make sure that there is no leakage of post-mortem blood from the stitched wounds, sometimes, minor leakage of blood tinged body fluid can happen. The chances of such leakage become high when bodies are being transported for long distances as it had happened in the Loya case.

The court made it clear that the petitions of Congress leader Poonawalla and others (represented by legal luminaries such as Dushyant Dave, Indira Jaising, Prashant Bhushan and others), though purportedly filed in the public interest, were actually meant to promote their "political agenda". In their attempt to seek "justice" for Loya, the petitioners and intervenors went so far as to "launch a frontal attack on the independence of the judiciary" which in the court's view, prima facie constituted criminal contempt. The court decided not to press the charge of contempt because "the credibility of the judicial process is based on its moral authority".

The Loya death case exemplifies that upon harbouring suspicion about a matter of concern to the public the Congress party could go to any extent, take on anyone—no matter what the repercussions. Crossing swords with the Supreme Court of India is a small matter for those who in the past tangled with the world's only superpower, alleging that the US might have a hand in Rajiv Gandhi's assassination. Not too long ago, in February 2017, the passing away of former minister E Ahamed after he suffered a heart attack while attending Parliament caused Congress leaders to spin or promote various conspiracy theories. Leader of Opposition in Rajya Sabha, Ghulam Nabi Azad, said his party had information that Ahamed passed away 'much earlier' than declared. Even as senior officials at RML Hospital refuted the allegations, Congress MP KC Venugopal gave notice for an adjournment motion to discuss the matter in the House. In his notice, Venugopal said: 'The unethical approach from the hospital officials and the government towards veteran parliamentarian Shri E Ahamed and his family members during his last hours has created anguish and concern among the people in the country…we need an impartial investigation.'[6] Rahul Gandhi himself protested in Parliament precincts in favour of an inquiry.

In total contrast we have the example of Lal Bahadur Shastri, the Prime Minister of India, dying in suspicious circumstances and yet the Congress government stonewalled all attempts to have the matter inquired into. Even today, their leaders and supporters do not utter a word about it, and when they do, they are dismissive. It stokes suspicions. In an article in 2017, former foreign minister K Natwar Singh stated that when Shastriji died, all hell broke loose. 'Was he poisoned? By whom? Enquires were instituted. All in vain. Why should Dr (RN) Chugh or any member of his personal staff have poisoned a beloved Prime Minister and that too in the Soviet Union?'[7] Earlier in September 2015, Kuldip Nayar told CNN-News18 that he was surprised that no post-mortem was done after Shashtri's death. He 'refused to comment on whether Indira Gandhi government deliberately didn't

6 **Congress says E Ahamed died 'much earlier', seeks probe**, *Indian Express*, 4 February 2017.

7 K Natwar Singh, **Jaya's death and conspiracy theories**, *The Tribune*, 12 February 2017.

want to take any action'.[8] The retort from Congress leader Shakil Ahmed was: 'It is known that Kuldip Nayar's writings were never in favour of the Gandhis.'[9] Was Ahmed Sattarov also a Congress-baiter then?

All the arguments that Congress gave in the case of Judge Loya could well have been given in the case of Shastri as well. The denial of information because it would harm our relations with Russia (successor state of USSR) is a pathetic excuse for a country whose Home Minister can stand up in Parliament and target the world's most powerful nation merely on the basis of an outrageous conspiracy theory. In the Subhas Bose case, the Congress government rejected the Mukherjee Commission's report based on robust circumstantial evidence, arguing that the eyewitness account was more important.[10] If that is so, what about the eyewitness accounts of Lalita Shastri and others, whose description of Shastri's body—the hole

---

8 Parikshit Luthra, **Surprised no post-mortem done after Shashtri's death, says former PM's media advisor Kuldip Nayar**, 26 September 2015. Accessed from: https://www.news18.com/news/politics/surprised-no-post-mortem-done-after-shashtris-death-says-former-pms-media-advisor-kuldip-nayar-1114202.html.

9 **It is known that Kuldip Nayar's writings were never in favour of the Gandhis**, 27 September 2015. Accessed from: https://www.news18.com/videos/india/it-is-known-that-kuldip-nayars-writings-were-never-in-favour-of-the-gandhis-shakil-ahmed-1115182.html.

10 Justice MK Mukherjee followed aphoristic saying, "Men may lie but circumstances do not."

on the back of the neck, "blood" spewing out, etc. ran contrary to what was given out officially? Why should we not believe Shastri's kin when they say that after his belongings were sent back to them they discovered a concealed note from him that read, "I have been betrayed"? Shastri was all smiles when the Tashkent accord was signed earlier in the day. So what was the betrayal about?

The way forward for the Shastri matter should be similar to what happened in the US following the release of Oliver Stone's *JFK*. Suggesting that the CIA had a hand in the President's assassination, the movie at the end underlined that the records relating to the case were being held secret. This led to much commotion, which resulted in the enactment of the landmark JFK Records Act of 1992. The act established an independent Assassination Records Review Board to smooth out the process of declassification of all assassination-related records. In compliance with the board's directive, many US departments and agencies released their records. While releasing the CIA files, its then director Robert Gates made an emotional statement: 'The only thing more horrifying to me than the assassination itself is the insidious, perverse notion that elements of the American government—that my own agency—had some part in it. I am determined personally to make public or to expose to disinterested eyes every relevant scrap of paper in CIA's possession in the hope of helping to dispel this corrosive suspicion....I believe I owe that to his memory.'[11]

Most documents relating to the Kennedy assassination case were thus released in this way. One bunch of intelligence records remained classified till they were released in 2017. The declassified files touch upon so many aspects, including Russian fears that they were getting blamed for the assassination. "Secrecy begets suspicions, which can metastasize into belief in conspiracy of the most awful sort", noted a US government report of 1997 on reducing secrecy.

May be a concerted effort can be undertaken now in India to resolve the Shastriji death controversy once and for all. Here's how it should happen:

The Government of India should set up a committee comprising top officials from Home, External Affairs, Defence, Health Ministries, as well as IB, R&AW and CBI—something on the lines of Multi-Disciplinary Monitoring Agency (MDMA) set up to probe the fictional "larger conspiracy" (read "American hand") in the Rajiv Gandhi assassination case. To be led by the Principal

11 John Aloysius Farrell, **Release Of CIA's file on Oswald reveals little new**, *Boston Globe*, 13 May 1992.

Secretary to the Prime Minister, this committee should be tasked to produce a report in a time-bound manner detailing the manner of Shastri's death, how the tragedy was handled, the validity of the claims that the death was not natural, etc. The committee should take on record statements of members of Shastri's family and others who witnessed the events in 1966. Some of the diplomats, intelligence officers and others from that period are still with us.

The committee should also consult forensic pathologists and other experts after furnishing them official statements, pictures, records, statements of those who saw Shastri's body with a view to get a sense whether the condition of his body was consistent with the manner of his death as stated officially. If Bhanwari Devi's remains can be sent to the FBI in America, why not seek their help over the Shastriji riddle? The FBI should be consulted because assuming such a test is carried out in India and the findings turn out to be contrary to what the Indira Gandhi government gave out, allegations of bias would be levelled in no time. On 2 April 2018, before the Supreme Court order came out, the Congress party fanned a conspiracy theory that held that "the post-mortem conducted on the dead body of deceased Judge BH Loya was manipulated under instructions from a doctor who is related to

Maharashtra Cabinet Minister (belonging to the BJP)".[12] When bias can be imputed to the Chief Justice of India for reasons political, would forensic experts be spared?

The compelling reason I think the Shastri matter must be taken up with the FBI is that I personally communicated with several doctors over the question—whether or not the state of Shastriji's body was consistent with the manner of his death as officially announced? Verbally, just about everyone said they sensed foul play. This was different from what CP Srivastava gave out after consulting Iain West. The problem was not with this leading British forensic pathologist, but how the case was presented to him. Dr West applied his mind on the details which essentially represented the official view of Shastri's death. And yet, even with this one-sided picture, West felt that "without a post-mortem examination and toxicological studies, it is impossible to say absolutely that no poison was administered", though he saw all signs of a heart attack—because that's what the official account stated. When I approached the experts, I laid before them information not only from the official side, but also what

12 **Death Most Foul: Judge Loya's Post-mortem Tampered**, Accessed from Congress party's official site: https://www.inc.in/en/in-focus/death-most-foul-judge-loyas-post-mortem-manipulated.

Shastri's family stated, along with the pictures of Shastri's body taken both at Tashkent (where the body was normal) and later in Delhi (where the body appeared dark bluish and bloated).

Whatever I could gather, from official records to what I heard from Shastri's family members (most importantly the statement Lalita Shastri gave to *Dharmyug*), I weaved into a precise note for the perusal of the experts. This note detailed the last-ditch efforts made by senior Soviet doctors and Dr Chugh in Tashkent to save Shastri's life; medicines pumped into his body, and how his body was embalmed after they failed to save him. The embalming liquid consisting of three litres of pure spirit, one litre of formalin and 200 grams of Urotropine was introduced through an incision into the femoral artery in the inguinal part of the body (corresponding to the groin area). But when the body was seen by family members a few hours later, the face and upper part of body had turned dark bluish. The face was swollen, almost dark, and on both sides of the forehead, on the temples, there were white marks. The body felt very hard when touched and it had bloated so much that, in order to perform the last rites, the vest had to be torn off. His kurta could be removed only with difficulty. There was a hole at the back of the neck from which "blood" was oozing and the sheets, pillows and the clothes were all soaked in "blood". There was also a cut mark on the stomach where sticking plaster had been pasted.

The question I then posed was: 'Is the condition of Shastri's body, as seen in the pictures and described by his family, consistent with the official description of his death and the subsequent embalming process?' I also supplied the following for consideration of the experts:

> Family members and others alleged that the death was not natural, that it was caused by some sort of poison (possibly placed in a thermos flask containing water) and that embalming was done to fudge the tell-tale signs of poisoning. For the record, we know now that Russians themselves suspected poisoning soon after Shastri died and that they offered to carry out a post-mortem, which was declined by then Indian govt. According to available information, in those days in USSR extreme care was taken to ascertain the cause of death, particularly in cases of suspected poisoning, accidental deaths and murder. In case of suspicions of poisoning, a complete chemical examination was made of all organs and in some instances organs were sent to bacteriological institutes for examination. As a layman I am not very sure whether embalming done by a team of qualified doctors would

reduce Shastri's body to such a state barely hours after he died. The Soviets were experts in embalming. Vladimir Lenin's corpse[13] is in pretty good shape till date.

Three experts made observations on the basis of my note. The first was Prof Dr Soumya Chakraborty (MS Anatomy, FAIMER USA), a reputed anatomist, and embalming as well as bioethics expert who is professor and head of anatomy department at ESI PGIMSR Joka, Kolkata. Dr Chakraborty consulted with experienced anatomists and forensic experts 'without disclosing the identity of the subject under study'. After getting their inputs, she made the following points:

- Six member team did embalming but none were experts in this field as per the qualifications/designations mentioned.
- Embalming fluid composition was not correct: Formalin only one litre and pure spirit only three litres. About six litres should be the embalming fluid with formalin at least five litres.
- Time of embalming was not mentioned though it was freezing in Tashkent.

13 Pathologist Alexei Ivanovich Abrikosov embalmed Lenin's body shortly after his death in 1924.

- On arrival in India why post-mortem was not done? Post-mortem can be done even after embalming though embalming interferes with toxicological studies.
- Dark bluish discoloration of face and upper part of body: Bluish discoloration means reduced hemoglobin which further indicates either poisoning or asphyxial death[14] leading to cyanosis[15] and histotoxic anaemia.[16] Usually it is more bluish in dependent parts of body though early bluish discoloration is observed in bulbar conjunctiva[17] and lips.
- White marks on temple: Contract pallor due to spectacles or cap indicate lack of blood accumulation.
- If embalmed properly, body should not feel hard when touched in freezing temperature in Tashkent.

---

14 Types of asphyxial deaths include hanging, strangulation, choking, drowning, etc.

15 Bluish or purplish discolouration of the skin.

16 According to Wikipedia, histotoxic hypoxia is 'the inability of cells to take up or use oxygen from the bloodstream, despite physiologically normal delivery of oxygen to such cells and tissues. Histotoxic hypoxia results from tissue poisoning, such as that caused by cyanide (which acts by inhibiting cytochrome oxidase) and certain other poisons like hydrogen sulfide (byproduct of sewage and used in leather tanning)'. Histotoxic hypoxia can lead to a condition called histotoxic anemia, which is marked by loss of red blood cells in blood, which, in turn, could be due to poisoning.

17 Conjunctiva is the moist membrane which coats the inner surfaces of the eyelids. Bulbar conjunctiva is that part of the conjunctiva which covers the outer surface of the eye.

Either death happened much earlier or it was a case of improper embalming.

- Hole in back of neck: May be misidentified bullet shot with trapped bullet inside or stab injury. However it was not blood oozing, rather it was altered colour embalming fluid oozing.
- Plaster in region of stomach is probably the place for femoral artery where embalming was done.
- After death, within two hours starts post-mortem hypostasis[18] which gets over in 4-6 hours where bluish discoloration sets in.
- Bloating is a sign of putrefaction: There is accumulation of carbon dioxide and water with organisms decomposing. During summer, putrefaction is between 12-24 hrs and bloating occurs in 24-36 hours in summer while in freezing or cold temperature it occurs after 48 hrs and beyond.
- Why organs were not sent for post-mortem chemical analysis; if not in Russia they could have been sent in India. For chemical analysis, organs, including blood, are sent in forensic chemical analysis laboratories and not in bacteriological institutes since bacteriological

---

18 Accumulation of blood in the lower parts of the body or organs under the influence of gravity.

institutes can talk about organisms and not chemical poisoning cases.

Thus, in Dr Soumya Chakraborty words, 'as per the question raised, it can be concluded that':

- Poisoning cannot be ruled out. There is a probability of potential poisoning, but it cannot be established with the information provided.
- Embalming was inadequate and done to transport the body back to India. Since post-mortem was not done, embalming can fudge tell-tale signs of poisoning as it interferes with toxicological studies, though autopsy can be done even after embalming.
- Post-mortem should have been done since without post-mortem cause of death cannot be identified. Russia being so sensitive about post-mortem raises the question why it was not carried out in this case?
- If Soviets were experts in embalming why embalming was not done properly in Shastriji's case?

Dr Sayan Biswas (MD in forensic medicine & toxicology, Faculty member in Nil Ratan Sircar Medical College, Kolkata) also did not rule out poisoning. Citing legal provisions, he underlined that in cases of a sudden death, it is mandatory to perform an autopsy, and even a second autopsy if required. He also indicated that the quantity of embalming fluid used to preserve Shastri's body was inadequate. 'Approximately 10 litres of the arterial fluid is prepared for an average adult of 65-70kg weight.' Swellings may appear in case there is an overfilling of tissues—which was not the case with Shastri as far less fluid was used and so the swelling couldn't have been the result of overfilling.

Dr Biswas stated that post-mortem hypostasis (bluish-purple or purplish-red discoloration) may occur if the head is kept lowered during the embalming process, which again indicates a botched-up procedure. The white patches that appeared on Shastri's body were "vibices"—a narrow linear mark or streak—which is the result of embalming fluid not reaching a certain area due to some pressure.

More importantly, Dr Biswas dwelt on "suspicion of introduction of substances causing derangement of the physiological systems", which in this instance means a possible attempt to conceal signs of poisoning through a shoddy embalming process not expected from Soviet Russia in ordinary circumstances.

An "ideal homicidal poison" is one that can simulate the signs and symptoms of a natural disease and also which can hardly be found in autopsy or even in putrefaction. Dr Biswas gave example of flowering plants known as aconitum, or more commonly "queen of poisons". 'From aconitum plant, a powerful alkaloid can be produced known as aconitin, which has been considered as one of the ideal homicidal poisons. Aconite has a bitter taste like *katha* (catechu) which can be introduced through paan (betel leaf) and also through tea; being classified as a cardiac poison, it mimics and also causes the features of myocardial ischemia and various arrhythmias.'[19]

Embalming, Dr Biswas noted, 'completely destroys cyanide, alcohol and many other substances' and 'determination of the presence of many of the alkaloids and organic poisons becomes very difficult.' Regarding the hole in the posterior part of the neck, he mentioned that cerebro-spinal fluid (CSF) or the fluid circulating in between the membranes of brain and spinal cord constitutes 'an important specimen for post-mortem toxicological analysis.' While CSF analysis is carried out to diagnose medical disorders that affect the central nervous system, it can also be performed in the course of forensic investigations to identify the presence of drugs or poisons in the bodies of murder, accidental overdose or suicide victims.[20] The normal procedure to collect from

19 Myocardial ischemia occurs when blood flow to heart is reduced, leading sometimes to heart attack. Arrhythmia relates to irregular heartbeats.

20 Cerebrospinal Fluid (CSF) Analysis. Accessed from: https://medical-dictionary.thefreedictionary.com/Cerebrospinal+Fluid+(CSF)+Analysis.

or introduce anything to the fluid, Dr Biswas states, is 'to puncture the intervertebral space between the 3rd and 4th or 4th and 5th lumber vertebrae situated at waist region (posteriorly).' However, a 'usual and safe alternative method is a lateral cervical[21] puncture under such circumstances.'

(A note by Dr Biswas is at Appendix 1)

The third expert to apply his mind on the details furnished by me was Dr Ajay Kumar Gupta, a reputed forensic pathologist who served as head of the department of forensic medicine at both Calcutta Medical College and Calcutta National Medical College. Dr Gupta (75) felt that it looked like a case of poisoning on the face of it, and wondered why this possibility was not excluded through a proper post-mortem examination.

> It is not only well-known to attending doctors, but also to all the concerned politicians and government officials that in all cases of sudden deaths of an old person above 50/60 years, it is not at all possible to decipher/declare the actual cause of death and its manner suddenly under a highly critical/peculiar/suspicious circumstances, in

21 Lateral cervical region is a region of the neck.

> in a foreign country. From the photographs of dead Lal Bahadur Shastri, a strong suspicion arises that it may be a case of death due to some vegetable poison acting on the heart, which can be excluded only by a thorough and detailed Medico-legal post-mortem examination. It is not clear why the wife and sons of Shastriji did not personally go to the Officer-in-Charge of the local Police Station, and lodge a written request for holding post-mortem examination.

The fear of poisoning thus emerging as a likely reason for Shastriji's death prompted me to further consult Dr Nirmalya Roychowdhury, a member of American Board of Internal Medicine who practices in Seattle (United States) and in Kolkata, about the types of homicidal poisons and how they bring about death. Dr Roychowdhury stated that an 'ideal homicidal poison is expected to have the following properties— it is undetectable, water soluble, odourless, colourless, tasteless, and effective in very small dose and most importantly, its effect mimics a natural disease.'

He added, 'Though there is no ideal, undetectable poison, the toxic agents that satisfy the requirements and therefore, have been used repeatedly in different homicidal cases, particularly political homicides all over the world are—arsenic, cyanide, aconite, Polonium 210, Thallium, ricin and oleander.' An example is the sudden death of Palestinian leader Yasser Arafat. He fell ill in October 2004 with a mysterious illness presenting vomiting and other gastrointestinal symptoms. Teams of doctors from Palestine, Egypt and Tunisia treated Arafat for days without any success. Eventually he died in early November. No post-mortem examination was done either in France on in Palestine at that time. In 2012, with the permission of his widow Suha, Arafat's body was exhumed by the Palestinian authorities. A thorough forensic investigation was done. Study results almost proved beyond reasonable doubt that he was poisoned with Polonium 210, Dr Roychowdhury states, adding, 'I think for any person who is going to be cremated and not buried, the authorities need to be even more skeptical as the option of exhumation and examination in future does not exist.'

In case aconite is ingested, death usually occurs within a few hours. 'Initial symptoms are neurological such as seizures, gastrointestinal such as vomiting, followed by numbness in the mouth and face. Soon cardio vascular symptoms develop as bradycardia, hypotension and ventricular arrhythmias leading to death.' The symptoms of oleander poisoning too 'give an impression of heart attack and cardiac arrest.' One of the most toxic, commonly grown garden plants in the world, oleander was also 'synthesised in the laboratory and reportedly used extensively in Russia and China historically.' Following ingestion, 'initial symptoms may be gastrointestinal like nausea and abdominal discomfort. But soon the heart is affected by arrhythmias followed by cardiac arrest.'

(A note by Dr Roychowdhury is at Appendix 2)

The sum total of the comments made by various experts appears to lend credence to Dahyabhai Patel's conjectural reconstruction of what happened after Shastri's death. He wrote that "it is as certain as anything can ever be in this murky business that Dr [Evgenia] Yeremenko had not the remotest connection with any foul play that may have taken place". He felt that "the fact that her signature is missing from the official Death Bulletin presented to Parliament by YB Chavan strongly suggests that she stumbled on something suspicious about Shastri's collapse and, because she was not in on the plot, voiced her suspicions and had to be kept out of the way until the Indian delegation left for home. Once the Indians had gone there would be ample time for one of the 'senior doctors' who signed the bulletin (though they came well after life was extinct) to explain away whatever it was that had puzzled Dr Yeremenko and get her to append her signature to the 'Soviet' version of the bulletin".

> As for the mysterious "cuts" noted by so many people, if Dr Yeremenko did indeed discover something suspicious, she could well have made the "hole" at the back of the neck and the "incision like a plus sign" on the abdomen to draw off spinal fluid and visceral samples. Not being in the confidence of the KGB she would naturally assume an autopsy would be routine in a case like this. One can imagine the reaction of the KGB man planted among the "senior doctors" who now came on the scene. Well aware of the true reasons for Shastri's mysterious collapse but unable to undo the incisions, he could only try and hush up the matter as best he could by ordering the cuts to be taped up. Though all this is conjecture, it is at least more plausible than suggestions that the cuts were inflicted by injection needles!

Reverting to the proposed committee, it should get fullest support from the Prime Minister of India for the simple reason that the matter relates to the death of his predecessor. Therefore, in order to help the committee fulfill the task assigned, the Prime Minister should issue a clear direction to all the heads of relevant ministries, departments and agencies (especially R&AW and IB) that every scrap of record available to them relating to the death of Shastriji and all those who figured in the narrative of his death, like Dr Chugh, Jan Mohammed and TN Kaul, should be passed on to this committee. Record means information available on any format—electronic, paper, picture or microfilm. On their return to India, Shastri's staff, Ambassador Kaul, Foreign Minister Swaran Singh and others must have given detailed statements for the record. Earlier this year, senior journalist Prem Prakash observed that 'no one has seen till today any archive papers of Indian delegation's inner talks at Tashkent. Have those documents been destroyed? No one tells. The mystery continues.'[22]

The intelligence records are most crucial given India's world-level expertise in this field. The highly sophisticated manner in which surveillance was mounted on Netaji's family members makes similar effort in Nixonian America look amateurish. It went on and on for decades without anyone getting wind of it. But poor Richard Nixon lost his presidency due to a failed attempt by former

---

22 **"Come down your Prime Minister is dead"**—A first hand account of the night PM Shastri Died. Accessed from https://www.aninews.in/news/national/general-news/come-down-your-prime-minister-is-dead-a-first-hand-account-of-the-night-pm-shastri-died201801111841140001/.

CIA personnel to plant an eavesdropping device in the Democratic Party office in the Watergate complex. This would have been child's play for our sleuths who mastered the art of skullduggery, building up from where the wily British left. A former CBI director related an anecdote to me long ago. Pakistan's President Zia-ul-Haq came to India in 1987. He met President Giani Zail Singh, whose relations with Prime Minister Rajiv Gandhi were frosty. No sooner had they started talking at Rashtrapati Bhavan when Zail Singh, a former Home Minister (under whom the IB functions) quipped, *General saab diwaron ke bhi kaan hote hain.* (Walls have ears too, General). Zia got the cue and both stepped out into the Mughal Gardens.

Consequently, India's intelligence archives are said to have a fabulous collection. Every time former IB Chief and National Security Advisor MK Narayanan teased people with his 'I have a file on you' jibe, he was unknowingly paying a compliment to the richness of the documentation in the possession of India's spy agencies. It is difficult to believe that such cunning and shrewd people did not attempt to collect information related to Shastri's death or conspiracy theories about it. If files could be opened on Subhas Bose's kin, who were of zero consequence to New Delhi post-1947, if MPs could be spied upon just because they wanted to organise a function to welcome

Netaji's sword[23] being brought from Japan, there must be thick dossiers on Lalita Shastri, Raj Narain and others who were openly holding the government responsible for what happened in Tashkent.

If it is given out in future that there are no such dossiers or records, it would mean they were destroyed—as many of the important papers concerning Subhas Bose were destroyed by the Indira Gandhi government.[24] The absence of files would muddy the water further. It would be advisable that the PM's direction over the committee about the Shastriji matter should include clear instructions that all records to be sent to the committee should carry written declarations by the heads of concerned ministeries, etc. that the disclosure is full and nothing is held back.

23 According to a PMO file declassified in 2016, snooping was ordered on members of Parliament who were part of a reception panel constituted to receive Subhas Chandra Bose's sword in New Delhi in 1967. The Prime Minister's Secretariat (now PMO) instructed the then Intelligence Bureau director SP Varma to investigate the "composition of the committee, its aims and objectives" and whether Congress party was represented on this committee. It also sought information on what was proposed to be done with the sword in the Capital.

24 The most important of the destroyed file was No. 12(226)/56-PM (Circumstances leading to the death of Shri Subhas Chandra Bose). Opened in 1956, this file was destroyed in 1972 along with several other irrelevant files, even though the Manual of Official Procedure in force at that time stipulated that the files of historical importance, especially those relating to issues agitating the public mind, would be kept in office for 25 years and then sent to the National Archives. What makes this destruction completely illegal is that in 1972 a commission of inquiry was probing the matter of Netaji's death.

Missing records and those destroyed should also be accounted for. The death of a former PM of India cannot be taken lightly in view of charges that it was actually a murder.

Most importantly, the Prime Minister should make a public announcement freeing all serving and retired government officials, especially those with the intelligence services, from the provision of Official Secrets Act in the context of the Shastri death matter. For the sake of truth and justice, they should be exhorted to share their views with the committee without any fear of retribution.

Having taken these steps domestically, the Prime Minister should seek support from his counterparts in four friendly foreign nations who might have information relevant to the Shastri death matter. They should be requested to share information, especially the records of intelligence agencies. These nations could be told that while releasing their papers, they could censor the intelligence sources and the methods of intelligence collection—otherwise they would be wary of releasing them. To us, only the information matters. In 2003, after the Government of India flatly refused to try and access the secret US government records relating to Netaji's death using the Freedom of Information Act, I obtained two CIA records using the same act. Initially, the agency turned down my request because the release was likely to harm US interests. But eventually they were released when I appealed to them that it should be done for the sake of Bose's admirers the world over, including in America, with necessary censorship of the names of agents and the method employed to collect information.

Most likely, there would be great revulsion within our Government at the idea of releasing intelligence records concerning a sensitive matter. Variety of excuses would be cooked up to prevent India from seeking such records from other nations, due to the underlying fear of some dark secrets spilling out. Officers might say that we should not seek intelligence records from other countries because they might seek our records in turn. This was the pretext used to sabotage an attempt in the mid-1990s to ask the Russians about the KGB records related to Netaji. As a declassified record concerning the Netaji matter reveals, it was not "appropriate" for the Government to seek access to the intelligence archives because we would be "embarrassed were a similar request, on the basis of reciprocity, be made by the Russian government at a later stage". This was such a laughable excuse. India has for the last seven decades championed the need to follow the high ideals of Mahatma Gandhi whose life and teachings were all about truth and transparency. We must demonstrate to the rest of the world by our action, not merely by rhetoric, that we follow Gandhian precepts in letter and spirit.

Practically speaking, we should have no reservations in returning the favour of friendly foreign nations by giving them access to our intelligence archives because we have no skeletons to hide and, also, it is fairly common for friendly nations to exchange current, operational intelligence, leave aside records from a bygone era and that too something as poignant as the death of a head of government. A classic illustration was provided a few years ago by Prof Christopher Andrew, the world's most respected intelligence scholar and writer of the authorised history of the MI5, the British intelligence agency. He told the *DNA* of Mumbai in an interview that during the Nehru years the Intelligence Bureau had actually invited the MI5 'to come over and have a look at the records that the IB has collected on the Moscow subsidies to the Communist Party of India'.[25]

The first country to be approached over the Shastri matter should be the Russian Federation, the successor state of Soviet Russia. The approach to Russians at the highest level must be made with a solemn declaration that

25 G Sampath, **The Intelligence Bureau was closer to MI5 than to Nehru**, *DNA*, 2 May 2010.

India would be grateful for any information supplied and that no disclosure would be allowed to come in the way of the present friendly relations between the two countries. It goes without saying that the Soviets must have maintained a detailed account of Shastri's death in their archives. It would have included interrogation reports of Mohammed Jan and others by the KGB. After the controversy started in India that his death was not natural, it was obvious the Soviets would keep an eye on it.[26] All those records must be lying intact in present-day Russia as there would be no sense in destroying them.

Uzbekistan should be the second country to be approached. There is a strong possibility that they may have some records from the Soviet era relating to what happened in Tashkent. It is possible that some people who witnessed the events in January 1966 are alive today. It is also possible that some left their accounts, either officially or at a personal level, with bearing on Shastri's end. Dr Uktam Aripovich Aripov (died 2001), the leader of the

---

26 In 2005, Justice MK Mukherjee, then probing the Subhas Bose matter, visited the Russian State Archive of Socio-Political History. He was accompanied by some others, including Pioneer senior editor Udayan Namboodiri. The director of the archive told Mukherjee that they had one file on Subhas. When seen, it turned out to have contained the Tass reports on Bose-related news reports published in Indian, British and Chinese newspapers for the period 1942-1956. Namboodiri wondered why "Russia was so interested in Indian media coverage on Netaji's disappearance till 1956."

team of doctors who tried to save Shastri's life and then embalmed his body, was a known person in the medical fraternity in Uzbekistan. Between 1971 and 1984, he was the rector of the Tashkent state medical institute. He authored 460 scientific works.

Americans should be approached as well. Surely, the CIA and State Department have not declassified everything related to the Tashkent summit on which they were keeping a close eye. The Americans are unlikely to turn down a sincere Indian request. They are beholden to us for our assistance in locating the remains of their war dead in India. *The Washington Post* reported in 2012 how "India agreed…to allow American military teams to search the Himalayan mountains for the remains of hundreds of US service members who went missing during World War II". US Defense Secretary Leon Panetta was reported as saying: 'This is a humanitarian gesture by a government with whom we share so many values. The ability to return heroes to their loved ones is something that America deeply, deeply appreciates.'[27]

After Americans, it was the British who had the best intelligence on the Soviet Union. So, our Prime Minister

27 Rama Lakshmi and William Wan, **India allows U.S. to recover World War II airmen's remains from the Hump**, *The Washington Post*, 6 June 2012.

should also request his British counterpart to share with India whatever information they have concerning Shastri's demise in Tashkent. Over the years there were so many who defected to the West with so much of information, now available with the intelligence archives of the UK and other countries. A well known case is of former KGB archivist Vasili Mitrokhin, who brought with him thousands of pages containing his notes of secret records—the biggest counter-intelligence bonanza of the post-world war period. The British shared these notes with several friendly countries. It is possible they might have shared with us because, as rightly commented by late B Raman, who used to be Additional Secretary in R&AW, 'after the US and Canada, the British intelligence has had the longest history of liaison relationship with the Indian intelligence since 1947.'[28]

So we can always ask the British whether, either in the Mitrokhin notes or any of their holdings, there is anything relevant to the Shastri death issue. Records declassified in 2015 by the British themselves show that Indian IB was sharing with them information relating to Subhas Chandra Bose after Independence. When we can spy on our people

---

28 **B Raman, Mitrokhin: More questions than answers**, 28 September 2005, http://www.rediff.com/news/report/raman/20050928.htm.

and share intelligence about them with our former colonial masters, there should be no shame in asking them about information relating to Shastri's death.

The information thus gathered from all sources should be utilised by the committee to produce a report. This report then should be made public by the Government along with all foreign and domestic records. By doing so, the Government would at least be laying to rest the charge of not being transparent enough over the death of a much loved Prime Minister.

I sincerely want to believe that Shastriji died a natural death, but available information compels me to draw a conclusion to the contrary. Nightmarish scenarios start rolling in my mind's eye—just as they did in Dahyabhai Patel's mind decades ago: It is pitch dark and very cold. Shastriji gets up feeling as if life is being sapped from him. He turns on the light but has a seizure and it is dark all over again. He regains his senses and now has a premonition that something wrong has been done to him. He looks around and sees the thermos, his spectacle case, his pen and a writing pad. Quickly, he scribbles his apprehension on a small piece of paper and slips it into his spectacle case.

I hate to think that our great Prime Minister's soul was never at peace after what happened in Tashkent. Could it be the reason why countless of us are restless still?

Appendix i

Note by Dr Sayan Biswas

i. Inquest is the inquiry or investigation into the cause of death where the death is sudden, suspicious and unnatural. According to the World Health Organisation (WHO), "Death is said to be sudden or unexpected when a person not known to have been suffering from any dangerous disease, injury or poisoning is found dead or dies within 24 hours after the onset of terminal illness". In India, it is mandatory to perform an autopsy upon any death falling under the provisions of inquest as per 174/176 CrPCs, 1973, and so on. There are even provisions of exhumations and second autopsy too.(1, 3)

ii. In order to preserve dead bodies, two types of embalming procedures are normally practised: Arterial embalming, where the embalming fluids are given through the various arteries; and Cavity embalming, where the fluid is introduced in the various body cavities through a trocar. Another form of embalming procedure sometimes mentioned is Hypodermic embalming in which a hypodermic needle is introduced behind the ear i.e. mastoid region. (2) Femoral artery is a very approachable area for Arterial embalming and femoral vein is used for drainage too, while, two inches above and two inches left to the umbilicus are the two usual points where the trocar is being introduced for Cavity embalming.

Hyperfluidity of blood occurs normally after death due to fibrinolysis i.e. degradation of the component fibrin which is required for normal coagulation. Embalming causes more fibrinolysis. Clotting is the main hindrance in embalming procedure and that is why anticoagulants like oxalates and citrates are used. Port-site oozing (purge) is also not uncommon. (2) The injection and drainage procedures go simultaneously in the embalming. The head may be lowered if needed and so should be the foot end to ensure that the fluid reaches the peripheral parts. (2) If the head end is kept lowered, being the dependent part of the body, hypostasis may cause staining of the face and the upper part of the body simulating congestion.

Post-mortem hypostasis is the bluish-purple or purplish-red

(due to de-oxy-haemoglobin) discoloration, which appears under the skin in the most superficial layers of dermis (rete mucosum)of the dependent parts of the body after death, due to capillo-venous distension.(3)

So, after death, it is the stasis of the deoxygenated blood in the dependent parts within the distended capillaries of the superficial skin which causes discoloration. Any pressure which prevents the capillaries from filling, such as the collar band, waist band, turbans, belts even the wrinkles in the clothes etc. —such areas remain free from colour and are seen as strips or bands called "vibices".(3)

There is six to seven litres of blood in the vascular system of an average body. This accounts for approximately 8 per cent of the total body weight. Usually, (apart from the cavity fluid) the arterial fluid injected should be equal to the blood volume of the deceased to ensure effective embalming. 'It is always better to over-embalm than to under-embalm a body.' Approximately 10 litres of the arterial fluid is prepared for an average adult of 65-70 kg weight. The amount of cavity fluid of a 70 kg deceased person should be at least one litre.(2) There is always danger of overfilling tissues and causing swellings, and for this reason the embalmer must continuously observe and be present while injection is in progress.' (2)

iii. With regard to the suspicion of introduction of substances causing derangement of the physiological systems, it is pertinent to mention that Georgi Markov, a Bulgarian journalist, was assassinated on a London street in September 1978 via micro-engineered pellets containing ricin, a potent toxalbumin found in Castor seeds. The pellets were fired into his leg from an umbrella wielded by someone associated with the Bulgarian Secret Service. It has been speculated that they asked the KGB for help. (4) Likewise, from aconitum plant, a powerful alkaloid can be produced known as aconitin, which (since ancient times in China) has been considered as one of the 'ideal homicidal poisons'. (3, 5)

An ideal homicidal poison is one which is cheap and easily available; deadly, having the same gustatory characteristics in comparison with the normal foods or drinks, simulating the signs and symptoms of a natural disease, and also which can hardly be found in autopsy or even in putrefaction. (3, 5)

Aconite (*meetha zahar*) has a bitter taste like *katha* (catechu) which can be introduced through paan (betel leaf) and also through tea. Being classified as a cardiac poison, it mimics and also causes the features of myocardial ischemia and various arrhythmias.(3, 5)

In any case of suspected poisoning, it is mandatory to preserve the samples taken from the person affected with the poison, otherwise the treating physician is held responsible for the omission and withdrawal of evidence under the provisions of Section 201 and 202 of the IPC. There are autopsy guidelines specifying which organs must be preserved, and also how they should be preserved to be forwarded to Forensic Science Laboratories, maintaining the chain of custody.(3)

iv. Drugs used in resuscitative measures: Micoren (Prethcamide) is used in chronic ventilatory failure. (6) Mephentermine sulphate is used as a cardiac stimulant. The circulatory drugs which are used in ante-mortem or peri-mortem period can cause poor distribution of fluids during the embalming procedure and accumulation of more waste-filled tissues. (2) 'Embalming completely destroys cyanide, alcohol and many other substances. Determination of the presence of many of the alkaloids and organic poisons becomes very difficult.' (3)

v. The hole in the posterior part of the neck: Cerebro-spinal fluid (CSF) or the fluid circulating in between the membranes of brain and spinal cord are an important specimen for post-mortem toxicological analysis and since it is a very important body fluid it can also reflect various maladies even in the living. The normal procedure to collect from or introduce anything to the fluid, is to puncture the intervertebral space between the 3rd and 4th or 4th and 5th lumber vertebrae situated at waist region (posteriorly). However, there are situations where lumbar puncture is either contraindicated or technically not feasible. The usual and safe alternative method is a lateral cervical puncture under such circumstances.

Lateral cervical puncture involves the placement of a spinal needle into the C1-C2 interspace, posterior and anterior to the vertebral artery. The vertebral artery ascends through the foramina in the transverse processes of the cervical vertebrae beginning at the sixth cervical vertebra. Inserting the needle 1 cm anterior to the tip of the mastoid process (the hard globular bony prominence behind the ear) and 1 cm posterior from that point will avoid puncturing the vertebral artery.(7)

References:

1. *A Textbook of Medical Jurisprudence and Toxicology*, Modi JP; 24th edition, 2011, Lexis Nexis publication, Nagpur.
2. *Embalming Principals and Legal Aspects* , Ajmani ML; Reprint in 2009, Jaypee bothers, New Delhi.
3. *The Essentials of Forensic Medicine and Toxicology*, Reddy KSN, 33rd edition, 2014; Jaypee bothers, New Delhi.
4. https://en.wikipedia.org/wiki/Georgi_Markov
5. *Modern-Medical-Toxicology*, Pillay VV; 4th edition, 2013; Jaypee bothers, New Delhi.
6. https://www.ncbi.nlm.nih.gov/pubmed/4913786
7. https://accessemergencymedicine.mhmedical.com/content.aspx?bookid=683&sectionid=45343760

Appendix ii

A note on homicidal poisoning

—By Dr Nirmalya Roychowdhury

Any instance of a person dying on foreign soil is considered a legal matter by both that foreign country as well as the home country of the deceased. If there is evidence of direct physical trauma, such as an automobile accident, or traumatic homicide, then a post-mortem examination is done. If there is no obvious trauma and the deceased was not suffering from any serious inter-current illness, then the case is considered to be of poisoning unless proven otherwise. A post-mortem investigation needs to be done in such cases under the international law. A proper forensic examination is necessary to determine if it is a case of natural death, suicide or homicide.

When it comes to poisoning, an ideal homicidal poison is

expected to have the following properties— it is undetectable, water soluble, odourless, colourless, tasteless, and effective in a very small dose and, most importantly, its effect mimics a natural disease. Though there is no ideal, undetectable poison, the toxic agents that satisfy the requirements, and thereby, have been used repeatedly in different homicidal cases, particularly, political homicides all over the world are—arsenic, cyanide, aconite, Polonium 210, Thallium, ricin and oleander.

Some of these toxins can be administered in small dosages over many days and lead to slow death over a period with symptoms of a natural illness. The classic example of this is arsenic. A single dose of Polonium or Thallium will also cause death over a period with symptoms mimicking the course of a natural disease. On the other hand, some of the toxins like cyanide, aconite, oleander, ricin and botulinum will lead to rapid toxicity and onset of symptoms. Rapidity of fatality depends on individual toxin and dosage administered.

There is a history of many political assassinations using arsenic. The most well-known victim was King George III of Great Britain. Recently, an ex-KGB spy Alexander Litvinenko was poisoned by polonium 210 in London. There is a suspicion among many that Palestinian leader Yasser Arafat was also poisoned with this deadly poison. Arafat fell ill in October 2004 with a mysterious illness presenting vomiting and other gastrointestinal symptoms. Teams of doctors from Palestine,

Egypt and Tunisia treated him for days without any success. Eventually he started developing evidence of disseminated intravascular coagulation, commonly abbreviated as DIC. At this stage, Arafat was transferred to Percy Hospital in Paris. At Paris multiple specialists from different disciplines started investigations and treatment. No one understood the source of this illness. Arafat's platelet count dropped and in a situation of DIC he was at a very high risk of any form of hemorrhage. He had a massive intracranial hemorrhage and died in early November after a month long struggle with this mystery illness. All efforts of doctors from multiple countries proved to be futile. Unfortunately, no post-mortem examination was done either in France on in Palestine at that time.

In 2012, with the permission of his widow Suha, Arafat's body was exhumed by the Palestinian authorities. A thorough forensic investigation was done with collaboration of multiple laboratories in France, Switzerland and elsewhere. Forensic studies including Polonium level in his bones were conducted. Study results almost proved beyond reasonable doubt that he was poisoned with Polonium 210. I think for any person who is going to be cremated and not buried, the authorities need to be even more skeptical as the option of exhumation and examination in future does not exist.

Aconite is a plant where all the plant parts are toxic, particularly the roots. This is source of a toxin called aconitine that opens tetrodotoxin sensitive sodium channels and delays cellular re-polarisation mechanism, thereby causing electro -physiologic disruption at the cellular level. Death usually occurs within few hours of ingestion. Initial symptoms are neurological such as seizures, gastrointestinal such as vomiting, followed by numbness in the mouth and face. Soon cardio vascular symptoms develop as bradycardia, hypotension and ventricular arrhythmias, leading to death.

The most commonly heard and presumed by masses as the most dangerous poison is cyanide, either in the form of potassium cyanide or sodium cyanide or hydrogen cyanide. Cyanide was used by Nazis frequently for suicide. Notable names are Heinrich Himmler and Adolf Hitler's wife, Eva Braun. Cyanide causes inhibition of cellular metabolism by inhibiting the mitochondrial enzyme Cytochrome C oxidase. This causes internal asphyxiation and histotoxic hypoxia leading to very quick death. Symptoms include severe apnea, cardiac arrest and coma with death following in few minutes. Very low dose exposure can cause generalised weakness, giddiness, vertigo, headache and confusion.

Oleander poisoning is a way to rapidly kill someone, where the symptoms will give an impression of heart attack and cardiac arrest. Oleander owes its profound toxicity to the compound oleandrin and nerine. Oleander has also been synthesised in the laboratory and reportedly used extensively in

Russia and China historically. This compound acts as cardiac glycosides inhibiting sodium—potassium ATPase. Onset of action is quite rapid. Initial symptoms may be gastrointestinal like nausea and abdominal discomfort. But soon the heart is affected by arrhythmias followed by cardiac arrest.